A WOMAN IN YOUR OWN RIGHT

Anne Dickson is a freelance psychologist, writer and trainer. She is recognised as a leading authority on women's development, assertiveness training and interactive communication. Her best selling, widely translated A WOMAN IN YOUR OWN RIGHT has become the core textbook for assertiveness trainers around the world. Together with 'Assert Yourself', a television series based on her work, it has helped to make the skills available to a broad population. She has extensive training experience in Britain, Scandinavia, Switzerland, Hungary, Africa and Japan.

A WOMAN IN YOUR OWN RIGHT

assertiveness and you

ANNE DICKSON

illustrated by Kate Charlesworth

QUARTET BOOKS

First published by Quartet Books Limited 1982
A Member of the Namara Group
27 Goodge Street, London W1T 2LD

Reprinted 1983 (three times), 1984, 1985 (twice), 1986 (twice), 1987
(twice), 1988 (three times), 1989, 1990, 1991, 1992, 1993, 1994,
1995, 1996, 1998, 1999, 2002, 2003, 2004, 2005, 2006, 2008, 2009,
2010 (twice)

British Library Cataloguing in Publication Data

Dickson, Anne
  A Woman in your own right.
  A. Assertiveness (Psychology)
  I. Title
  158.1 BF.575.A85

  ISBN 978-0-7043-3420-5

Phototypeset by
MC Typeset, Rochester, Kent
Printed and bound in Great Britain by TJ International Ltd, Padstow, Cornwall

For Margaret,
who showed me my self:
for my self
who showed immense courage

Contents

Acknowledgements

I cannot remember when the idea of writing this book first took shape. I know it was at Easter, last year in Yelping Hill, that Edward Brecher asked me what I was waiting for to get started. Since I couldn't come up with an answer, I did so. At Christmas, I showed him my enthusiastic and rambling first draft. Despite pressure to finish his own book, he gave me his time and generously shared his experience and expertise. I shall always remember my excitement at being introduced, under his informed care, to the disciplined art of writing.

All the women I have worked with in the many classes and workshops during the last five years have contributed to the content of the book: it is from their personally shared experience that I have drawn my examples and illustrations.

The women who have trained with me in the Redwood Women's Training Association have given me affection and encouragement as well as providing a powerful stimulus for me to clarify some complex and difficult issues.

I would also like to acknowledge the following people who have helped me along the way: Diana Athill, Silvia Burton Fairbrother, Liz Clasen, Lesley Garner, Nikki Henriques and Janet Law who each took the time to read various parts of the manuscript at different stages and gave me practical suggestions for improvement; Lindy Waller who typed the manuscript, despite a lot of personal inconvenience, and who has been an unfailing source of moral support; Katharine Hadley who pointed me in the right direction at the right time.

I would also like to thank all my friends, family and relatives whose loyalty and love have kept me going, especially Ron, Heidi and Dot who dissuaded me from giving up when I was ready to, and also Chucker who made her home available to me last summer providing me with the seclusion I needed to write the first draft.

Finally I would like to acknowledge the part played in all this by the lizard, the cat and the tree who bring magic into my life.

Preface

A Woman in Your Own Right is designed to help women who feel that they are too passive, too aggressive, or too manipulative. It explains how to be *assertive* instead. It is about basic patterns of behaviour and how to change them.

This book springs from my heartfelt commitment and my experience. For the past six years, I have been teaching assertiveness skills to women in classes and workshops all over England as well as in Ireland and Europe. I have witnessed first hand how mastering these skills has changed the lives of many women.

Women who come to these workshops are wealthy and poor, married and single; among them housewives, mothers, managers, artists, students, nuns and executives. Their experience of the changing world through the past decade has taught them that women need no longer sit quietly in the back seat but they have not yet learned *how* to move forward – to think for themselves, to speak out, to stand their ground. What they want and find in these workshops are techniques which help them handle difficult personal, social and professional situations.

This book is designed to make these techniques – assertiveness techniques – available to a wider audience.

I first became aware that methods of teaching assertiveness existed when I enrolled in an assertiveness class on a visit to America in 1976. On my return to England, I enthusiastically began to share with other women what I had learned and, in the process, learned much more about myself. I also learned more from the stream of books on assertiveness, all of them American (see Further Reading, page 158). *A Woman in Your Own Right* is a synthesis of what I have learned from my reading as well as my experience.

The skills taught in a basic assertiveness class include making clear, specific requests, learning how to say 'no', handling criticism – both on the receiving end and when you need to confront someone else; learning about body language; managing the expression of feelings, especially anger; receiving compliments; taking the initiative; building your self-esteem and improving your self-presentation.

A Woman in Your Own Right is not an attempt to duplicate the experience of a class, where the learning, humour and support are unique. This book provides an explanation of assertiveness techniques and skills for those women who cannot get to a class near their home or who simply prefer to try things out on their own. There are suggestions and exercises at the end of several chapters, which can be done alone or with a friend. Women who have already attended a class will find some new ideas and further stimulus to action.

I make no apology for the fact that this book is addressed primarily to women. I am confident, however, that the techniques here described can be equally useful to men, because I have presented them successfully to mixed classes. I have found that women are no more in need of assertiveness techniques than men – they simply need them differently.

Given our prevailing culture, women are, with obvious exceptions, in less powerful positions than men. This can be made into an overtly political issue – but that is not the purpose of this book. It is designed to help individual women in their own particular setting to live more assertively and powerfully. It provides simple, effective tools to accomplish this and, in some small measure, potentially to change the overall status of women in our society.

This book is written out of a profound love for women, a continued wonder at their courage and an unshakeable conviction that the techniques this book describes really work!

A Woman in Your Own Right

When and Where to be Assertive

For six years I have been working with groups of women who have wanted to change their lives in some way. A few came to the classes with a clearly defined goal, but most stumbled blindly into the group, pushed by some dimly-felt awareness that all was not well in their lives. Before making improvements, they had to determine exactly what was wrong.

Many felt that they lacked control over their lives. There were a few good days in a year when they felt confident and secure, but mostly they worried . . . about what they said or did not say, whether they made the right or wrong impression. Many worried about how to avoid criticism or comparison. They felt buffeted from one person, or situation, to another – with little sense of management or choice.

Have you ever experienced similar feelings? Just occasionally, or often, or almost always? The questions which follow will help you begin to identify the situations which you would like to handle more successfully. Identifying the circumstances in which you would like to respond differently is an excellent first step towards achieving change in your life.

Situations with strangers. How do you respond if you are sitting in a busy restaurant and a waiter ignores you? Do you sigh and tap your fingers on the table? Or do you ask your (male) companion why he doesn't do something? Or do you march out noisily, spitting a few choice remarks over your shoulder as you go? If the food served to you is congealed or long past its prime, or bears little resemblance to what you ordered, how do you respond? Do you complain by whining? Do you rudely denounce the establishment or the puny specimen of a waiter? Or do you swallow your dissatisfaction with your food and achieve a slight sense of revenge by not leaving a tip? And what if you have been served with exactly what you wanted, and are just about to tuck in, and someone at the next table lights up a cigar? Do you pucker your face and suffer through your meal? Do you create a stir by waving your menu wildly under his nose by way of a strong but silent message? Do you offer to negotiate a compromise?

How do you respond when you suspect you are being sold yesterday's bread or rotten fruit? Do you risk making a scene, or do you hold back, decide to swallow your feelings and allow your reservations to remain unexpressed? How do you react when you have been waiting for ages in a queue, or you are in a hurry, and a sweet little old lady barges in front of you? Does it make a difference if the person who barges in front of you happens to be a six-foot-four man with a belligerent manner? Do you risk stating your opinion and earning disapproving stares from others? How do you respond when you encounter an intransigent sales manager who suggests the article you are returning has shrunk or come apart through your own negligence? Do you get into a slanging match and leave in high dudgeon or do you lose heart – either way losing out on your rights as a customer?

If you have chosen to sit in a non-smoking compartment on a long train journey and a fellow passenger lights up a cigarette, do you seethe inwardly and wait for someone else to do something about it, or do you look around anxiously for the guard so you can report the offence, or do you confront the smoker? When faced with an unhelpful shop assistant who is more concerned with gossiping than your purchase problems, do you react like a sergeant major? Do you threaten to report her to the director of the store (whom you happen to know personally of course!), or do you ask for help, clearly or apologetically? A charming salesman has gone to a lot of trouble to unpack every possible article in search of what you want, and still nothing fits your requirements. Do you buy something anyway even though it is not what you want, simply so as not to appear ungrateful, or do you thank him for his assistance but decline to buy anything?

Situations with friends. A friend wants to borrow a record that you want to listen to yourself. Do you put aside your own needs, or pretend you don't own the record, or that you promised to lend it to someone else? Do you say 'no' or suggest a compromise? If you feel angry with the way someone has treated you, do you communicate your feelings, or do you hide them – and keep the person waiting an hour the next time you arrange to meet? If you have to negotiate where to meet or what film to see or where to eat, do you make your own preferences clear or are you pushed around or manipulated into a choice which you are really not happy with? If a friend persistently uses you as a shoulder to cry on and rings up just as you are settling down to watch a favourite television programme, do you turn the sound down but keep one eye on the box and the receiver tucked under your chin muttering 'uh uh' occasionally, do you listen patiently, wishing you could see your programme, or do you say that you are busy and could she ring back? If a friend who is important to you is the subject of malicious gossip in a group of mutual acquaintances, do you turn a deaf ear, do you hit out aggressively and put them in their place, or do you express how you feel and ask them to stop?

Situations at home. In your own home are you a martyr, a slave or a tyrant? How do you behave if everyone leaves the washing up, the cleaning, the tidying up to you? How do you respond when you want to say 'no' to a child's request for money or for friends to come and play? How do you respond if you want to say 'no' to a demanding relative who wants to pay you a visit at a busy or inconvenient time? How do you react when you feel affectionate and put your arm around your partner but find your partner is too preoccupied? What happens if your partner feels sexy but you are just not in the mood? Or if you feel sexy but your partner is reluctant? How do you respond to criticism about your appearance from a lover or a parent? Do you feel rejected or come back with an aggressive retort? If you want some privacy at home, how do you go about getting it? Do you feel you can set limits or that you should always be on call for your family? How do you confront an irritating habit in someone you love?

Situations at work. Consider how you respond to legitimate criticism from a superior. Do you fly off the handle? Do you deny it at all costs? Do you reach around for someone else to blame? Do you shift uncomfortably from one foot to the other, feeling about three years old? Do you adopt a pained expression and sulk for the rest of the day? Consider also how you respond to unfair criticism from a superior. How do you criticize a subordinate for continual lateness, or sloppy work, or dishonesty? Do you agonize and wait for ages, ask someone else to deal with the matter, attack the person with all guns firing at once when they are least expecting it, turn a blind eye, or even get another job?

How do you respond if your male boss makes a sexual joke or a pass at you? Do you launch into a tirade about male chauvinist pigs, pretend you did not hear, or do you just play along knowing that you can pull out and get your own back later? If you feel that your employer's demands exceed your contract unfairly, how do you cope? Do you arrange a discussion and assertively put your case? Do you just give in and groan under the extra load, or do a bad job out of spite? How do you handle nosy colleagues who persist in interfering in your private affairs? Do you tell them to mind their own business, or deflect them with some juicy gossip about someone else? How do you deal with a bossy, domineering colleague? Do you give as good as you get or do you avoid confrontation? Do you complain bitterly in private, or plan some secret revenge for being bullied?

If someone does a good piece of work or has put in extra time and effort, how do you respond? Do you just not notice, or do you take the time to give specific verbal credit? What happens if someone praises your work? Do you squirm self-consciously and say it was really nothing to do with you, or do you agree with them assertively? If someone admires your appearance, or a new outfit, how do you respond? Do you dismiss the compliment defensively?

Four types of behaviour

Having glanced at some typical situations, the next step is to identify the types of response described in the above examples.

There are essentially four ways to react to any difficult situation. These are best explained by presenting caricatures of four women who exemplify them: Agnes, Dulcie, Ivy, Selma.

I have used women's names because this book relates specifically to women, although the same descriptions could equally apply to men's behaviour. A word of caution: these are intended as caricatures with the express purpose of underlining the differences between the four types; in reality no such women exist. Each of us is aggressive, passive, manipulative and assertive in different situations. However, it is useful to separate them into four distinct characters as a way of beginning to untangle the overall confusion about how we behave. They can be used to pinpoint the line of action you take at any given moment.

First comes Agnes, the aggressive type. Although Agnes comes across loudly and forcefully, she often has little real self-esteem. She seeks personal aggrandizement through belittling the thoughts, values and capabilities of others. She cannot afford to consider another person's point of view because she is hell-bent on winning. She is always aware of the competitive element in a situation and needs to prove her superiority by putting others down. Faced with a threatening situation, she responds with an outright attack, aiming at the other person's vulnerable points. Her compulsive over-reaction often alienates those around her. She may provoke an aggressive response in return, but people usually feel instantly on the defensive in her company. She resorts frequently to verbal or even physical violence and abuse, leaving in her wake a trail of hurt and humiliated feelings. People often harbour resentment towards her but may be afraid to express this to her directly for fear of more of the same treatment.

Next comes Dulcie, the doormat, who represents the passive type. She makes ideal fodder for Agnes. While Agnes tends to opt in with a vengeance, Dulcie tends to opt out. She finds it difficult to make decisions and avoids taking responsibility for making choices in her life. Consequently, others are often forced into making decisions for her, which makes them frustrated and resentful. Dulcie prefers to see herself as a victim of unfairness and injustice, so she always finds something or someone else to blame. As she clings on to her hard-luck stories and stagnates in her passivity and resignation, she infuriates people around her – particularly those in close contact. They will probably feel guilty at first because they cannot do more to help her, to make her happier, or to ease her burden. But after a while, this turns to exasperation at her lack of willpower and her persistently negative outlook on life. She puts herself down continually, refuses to acknowledge any compliments, and spends a lot of time starting her sentences with 'If only. . .' She attributes to others the skills, talents, and good fortune that she was not lucky enough to be blessed with. Faced with any kind of confrontation, Dulcie cries and gives in, or runs away to avoid it.

Third in line comes Ivy. Ivy is indirectly aggressive. Whereas Agnes hits out with her weapons leaving obvious scars, Ivy's well-chosen barbs hit the mark but never leave a trace. As with her two companions, Ivy's behaviour stems essentially from a low self-esteem; this is why she can never risk a direct approach. She does not trust herself or anyone else. She is skilled at deceiving others; she needs to be in control and to manipulate those around her to

avoid rejection and hurt. She may appear to think highly of others, but they can often detect an undercurrent of disapproval. People around Ivy are confused and frustrated at never being able to pin her down. Her attack is concealed, unlike that of Agnes, and she will often deny her feelings and wriggle away. Her main weapon is guilt. With a marksman's precision she knows how to aim at that little guilt button in those around her, and she engineers people into all sorts of situations to get what she wants.

Do any of these behaviour patterns strike you as familiar? And if you did recognize yourself or someone else in the descriptions, what was your immediate response? You probably found yourself crowing with self-satisfaction as you recognized the faults and deeds of another! But the uncomfortable recognition of *yourself* may have made you wince with remorse and embarrassment.

It is easy to be judgemental – to be hypercritical of yourself and others. If you take a more compassionate and realistic viewpoint, you will see that what all three have in common is a lack of any real self-esteem. This usually reflects our experience as children. Perhaps Agnes, for example, had to prove herself superior in order to earn approval and love. She feels no real self-confidence in just being herself, so is very mistrustful of others. Maybe, Dulcie was criticized so often as a child, that she is now afraid to make a move or show her true feelings. The Ivy in us has learned that as a woman she must use whatever subtle devices she can. Direct, honest, straightforward behaviour has never been encouraged in the 'gentler sex'.

In reviewing aspects of your own behaviour which seem to you Agnes-like, Dulcie-like or Ivy-like, try not to make excuses, to justify or to blame. Simply notice *how* you tend to behave. Try to observe the essential person beneath the behaviour. Notice how the Agnes interacts with the Dulcie in you; how you swing from aggression to passivity and back again.

This seesaw is a common problem. Understandably, women find themselves frustrated and demeaned by a conventionally passive stance and so hurl themselves into the fray in an attempt to redress the balance of power. Unfortunately, they often tip the scales in the other direction. By domineering and insensitive behaviour, they end up alienating and punishing those who are close to them. Realizing that this is not what they want either, and usually overwhelmed with guilt, they try to compensate by taking conciliatory steps in the opposite direction. For many women, this to-ing and fro-ing in a cloud of uncertainty represents a major source of tension and discomfort.

It may come as a relief to know that there *is* an alternative: the *assertive option*. And, what is more, such skills can be learned – which is what this book is about. One of the main reasons we make such a mess of things is that we simply do not have the skills. We need precise skills to use in those very situations where we choose to discard the familiar for the unfamiliar, the dishonest for the honest, the role for the person. We need to know how to communicate our thoughts and feelings and needs, neither aggressively nor passively but assertively.

And so to Selma, the assertive woman. Selma respects herself and the people she is dealing with. She is able to accept her own positive and negative qualities and, in so doing, is able to be more authentic in her acceptance of others. She does not need to put others down in order to feel comfortable in herself. She does not believe that others are responsible for what happens to her. She acknowledges that she is in charge of her actions, her choices and her life. She does not need to make others feel guilty for not recognizing her needs. She can recognize her needs and ask openly and directly – even though she risks refusal. If she is refused, she may feel rejected – but she is not totally demolished by rejection. Her self-esteem is anchored deeply within herself; she is not dependent on the approval of those around her. From this position of strength, she is able to respond sincerely to others, giving herself credit for what she understands and feels.

Many women will identify mainly with one of these four stereotypes, others with two, and still others with all four of them at different times. It is interesting to see if you can identify a pattern in your own life. In what category would you put your mother or father? Sometimes an aggressive mother will encourage a passive daughter, or a passive mother an aggressive daughter, or an indirect mother an indirect or aggressive daughter.

Let me say again that to recognize is not to blame. No one is at fault; each of us has simply learned to cope in the best way we could, given the circumstances at the time. Once we can let ourselves off the hook of feeling bad or guilty about our behaviour, we can begin to see choices and make changes in our lives.

What is an Assertive Woman?

Change can be a frightening prospect. What does it mean to be assertive? More specifically, what does it mean to be an assertive woman? Many people believe that assertiveness training is only for shy, retiring violets who need to learn to be more outspoken and less afraid of a good fight!

Consider the popular stereotypes of what it means to be 'an assertive woman': the career woman who discards her softer qualities as she climbs the professional ladder (assertiveness becomes synonymous with being unfeminine and hard-nosed); or the domineering wife who nags her husband and children into submission (here assertiveness is confused with being overbearing and a bully); or the woman who always gets what she wants by using any means available to her (this time, assertive is taken to mean ruthless and self-centred); or the ardent feminist who loudly confronts a sexist gesture or remark (now assertive implies hostility and aggression, in particular towards men).

No wonder so many women worry about the consequences of changing when these are the only models available. They are in fact all descriptions not of assertive but of aggressive behaviour. No wonder that women fear that learning to be assertive will make them hard, uncaring, selfish and insensitive. But if these are not right, where do we look for a true idea of what it means to be an assertive woman?

There is of course no such person as a *completely* assertive woman; however assertive a woman may appear to be, you can be sure that in some area of her life she has difficulty in being assertive. We all have. You may look at a high-powered career woman with all the public features of success and competence and think the last thing she needs is assertiveness training – but maybe in private, she suffers from one unsatisfactory sexual encounter after another because of her inability to refuse unwanted advances. A woman who has no qualms about returning things to a store or making a big scene until she gets what she wants may well find it impossible at home to avoid being a slave to her family. A woman who is apparently in command and uninhibited in social situations may be easily demolished by criticism or quite unable to take the initiative to reach out to another person and show affection. A woman who is an exemplary organizer and always appears to be in charge may find it impossible to ask for her own needs to be met, to ask for help when she needs it herself.

Whatever the external image we present – highly confident or timid, very loud or very meek – we have times when we feel relaxed and comfortable and we feel that we cannot go wrong: we also all have our areas of anxiety and difficulty, when we feel vulnerable and less able to say or do what we really want to say and do.

Rather than present an assertive model which should be aimed for, it is more important to see how you can act more assertively in your own life. Below are sample situations which have occurred in assertiveness training classes where each woman has been encouraged to explore her own chosen area of difficulty and to discover for herself a more effective way of handling that particular situation.

Wendy, very proudly devoted to her new baby, was flustered by her well-meaning but over-enthusiastic mother-in-law. She felt overwhelmed by the endless advice on childcare: the best way to hold, the best time to feed, the best way to change nappies and so on. Wendy would continually swallow her irritation because she didn't want to risk provoking a family row. The assertive solution she found was to express her frustration in a way that allowed her to remain sensitive to the older woman's feelings while asserting her need to make her own decisions about the care of her child.

Helen, a secretary, had just started a new and challenging job. She had been looking forward to a rare chance to have lunch with a special friend who was in town just for the day. Just before noon, her employer handed her some urgent work and asked her, as a favour, to work through the lunch hour. She unhappily cancelled her lunch date and put on a brave face, not wanting to make an unfavourable impression when she was so new to the job.

In this case an assertive solution could have been a workable compromise, which means being able to negotiate around a conflict of priorities. This is an important aspect of assertive behaviour. She might have explained, in this case, that she had a lunchtime engagement which was important to her and which she would like to keep but that she would be happy to stay late that evening to finish the work before she went home.

Paula, living in a women's collective, felt unhappy about the refusal of some of the members to keep to a task-sharing rota which they had drawn up together and agreed upon. She had fallen into the habit of grudgingly doing more than her fair share of the household chores. Every now and then she would let out her resentment by way of moaning and sighing but nobody seemed to take the hint. The assertive option for Paula was to take the initiative and not play the martyr. In this case, it meant calling a meeting of all the members and confronting those concerned with a request for action from the whole group.

Denise, a retired schoolteacher, had been looking forward to a drive down to the coast for the day to enjoy some solitude and peace. The evening before, her bossy elder sister had telephoned and invited herself along for the ride. Denise always felt very intimidated by her sister and usually gave in to her demands. This time she lied and pretended she'd changed her mind. Although this worked, Denise felt uncomfortable and would like to have made an assertive refusal, saying a clear, firm 'no' to her sister and stating clearly her preference for spending the day on her own.

Sometimes, women would find that being assertive meant that they no longer went 'over the top' when they were angry but that they could express very strong feelings without losing control.

Working in a predominantly male world of radio technicians, Tricia felt offended by one of her colleagues who persisted in cupping his hands around her buttocks while making comments laced with sexual innuendo. In similar situations she had lost her temper and let rip with a torrent of abuse about men in general, with emphasis on the particularly inadequate specimen in front of her. Although she made her feelings clear, she did not like having to be quite so nasty into the bargain. She discovered an alternative which was to face her colleague squarely and tell him without screaming how angry she felt, how offensive she found his behaviour and to ask him to stop. She decided to follow this with a clear statement of intention that, if he didn't take her seriously, she would put in an official request to the department not to be allocated to work with him again.

An assertive action can also mean choosing to make a clear request in the first place rather than waiting for the inevitable to happen and then sulking about it afterwards.

Christine was faced with this kind of situation. By mid-afternoon on the day of her tenth wedding anniversary, she had heard nothing from her husband – no call, no card, no flowers, no mention at all. Her feelings of rejection and disappointment were growing by the minute. She considered settling down to wait for his return home so she would be ready to give him the cold shoulder treatment and make sure he'd feel very guilty for having forgotten. She was pleased to report that for once she felt she had been very assertive – she had phoned her husband at work and reminded him of the date. He had been a little taken aback and embarrassed at having forgotten but delighted when she asked what he would like to do to celebrate.

Some women find that being assertive means feeling confident in situations which normally they find intimidating. When we are faced with someone who for one reason or another has more power or a higher status that we do, it can be difficult to assert our rights as an equal.

Marion found this to be true for her. Her eleven-year-old daughter developed irregular but very bad headaches. Various local hospital tests indicated the need for a series of brain scans and she was advised to see a top neuro-surgeon in a London hospital. She was normally a forceful and outspoken woman but was obviously anxious about her daughter. She wanted to know how best to care for her and what the chances were of a brain tumour. Her anxiety about the status and manner of the consultant made her feel quite helpless: when her questions were dismissed, she found herself unable to persist. What she learned to do in an assertiveness training class was to keep calm and keep going! This depended on her maintaining her confidence despite her anxiety. Although the consultant was an expert and had more specific knowledge than she did, she could still assert her right to be treated as an equal human being, and could persist until he took her questions seriously and answered them.

These are some of the meanings of being assertive – a far cry from the aggressive stereotypes. But it nevertheless is a common confusion. People will believe that being assertive means you will get what you want all the time. This is not only unrealistic but also means that every interaction automatically becomes a question of winning or losing. This is competitive and aggressive which may be appropriate in other contexts but it is important to understand how different this is from being assertive. And, as always, we have a choice. Choosing to behave assertively may mean not getting exactly what you want but having to negotiate a compromise instead.

Sue, a non-smoker, found herself in the minority of four to one in a meeting at work. Ideally she wanted them all to stop smoking so that she wouldn't be bothered by the smoky atmosphere. She decided to express her discomfort assertively, neither shouting nor whining but expressing her wish for her colleagues to stop smoking during the meeting. Her colleagues were sympathetic but felt unable to get through the meeting without a cigarette – nor did they want to leave the meeting to smoke outside. On this occasion, they reached a compromise together which was for one person to smoke at a time and the window to remain open throughout the meeting. Sue didn't get exactly what she wanted, but she didn't compromise her self-respect. She felt that her wishes had been heard and considered, not over-ruled. If each person concerned feels acknowledged, this is usually a sign that an interaction has been handled assertively, not aggressively.

The above examples show that we are so used to just two positions – top dog and under-dog, the powerful and the powerless, that we forget there can be a middle path. The tension and effort needed to win does not allow you to develop a genuine respect for the needs, feelings or rights of others or yourself. This principle of equality is one of the most important hallmarks of assertive behaviour.

3
Setting the Scene

In the last chapter we looked at a few examples of the sort of situations that have cropped up in assertiveness training classes. Since the main aim of this book is to provide the reader with an opportunity to try out assertiveness techniques for herself, I have included, at the end of several chapters, suggestions and exercises which readers can use to explore for themselves without the aid of a class. There are exercises which can be done alone, and situations which can be set up to try with one other person or maybe even with a small group of people who are similarly interested in learning to be more assertive.

Exercise 1. Set aside fifteen minutes on your own. Take a pen and paper and sit down. Make a list of ten situations in which you would like to be more assertive. They can be taken from any area of your life – like those described in the first chapter – with people in shops or at home, with friends, the bus conductor, relatives, children, your neighbour, colleagues, your partner, your parents – anyone you come into contact with in the course of your life.

When you have the list in front of you, write down next to each situation how you behave now – aggressively, passively or manipulatively – (avoiding a situation altogether goes into the passive category): in other words do you behave more like Agnes, Dulcie or Ivy? You may find that you need to write down more than one category if you respond both aggressively *and* passively, for example, at different times.

If you have another fifteen minutes, go on to Exercise 2. If not then wait until you have the time. It does not matter if you leave it

(a) — as she first wrote them down:

Asking Veronica to replace a cup which she had broken, which was a gift.

Requesting people I live with to take their share of keeping the house tidy.

Requesting Barry to wash his used ash-trays ...

Asking Maureen not to smoke in the office.

Telling Hilary I feel let down by her not sending illustrations to a friend.

Asking friends to take care of/lend books I lend them.

Being firm with clients who I feel are asking me to take a course of action I don't want to take.

Expressing my anger directly with people I am close to.

Asking Tim to stroke/caress me whilst making love.

Responding assertively/spontaneously to non who have made patronising assumptions about women.

(b) — after she had put them in order of difficulty:

① Asking friends to take care of books I lent them. — AGGRESSIVE/

② Being firm with clients who feel are asking me to take a course of action. I feel resentful about doing. — AGGRESSIVE

③ Requesting people I live with to take their share of keeping the house tidy. — PASSIVE & AGGRESSIVE

☆ Asking V. to replace a cup she had broken, which was a gift to me. — PASSIVE

⑤ Requesting Barry to wash his used ash-trays. — PASSIVE

⑥ Asking M. not to smoke in the office. — INDIRECT

⑦ Telling Hilary I feel let down by her not sending illustrations to a friend. — PASSIVE

⑧ Asking Tim to caress me whilst making love. — INDIRECT

⑨ Responding assertively/spontaneously to non who have made patronising assumptions about women. — INDIRECT

⑩ Expressing my anger directly with people I am close to. — INDIRECT

One woman's list of problem situations (a) as she first wrote them down and (b) after she had put them in order of difficulty

1 DEALING WITH DOORSTEP SALES PEOPLE — *Fairly Passive.*

2 SENDING FOOD BACK IN RESTAURANTS. — *Embarassed, but do it.*

3 REFUSING DRY ALCOHOL IN SOCIAL SITUATIONS — *Aggressive*

4 WANTING PRIVACY — *Passive.*

5 ASKING FOR REPAYMENT OF A LOAN *Passive until overdue, then forced into being aggressive.*

6 COMPLAINING TO UPSTAIRS TENANT ABOUT LEVEL OF NOISE/FILTH IN HALL *Passive - difficult, because person already threatened to attack me.*

7 JUSTIFYING DOS & DONTS TO PROSPECTIVE TENANTS. — *Passive.*

8 UPSET BY RACIST/SEXIST COMMENTS — *Passive, then aggressive*

9 NEGOTIATING MONEY, PAYMENTS, RENT, SALARY. *Passive.*

10 CRITICISED UNJUSTLY BY A SUPERIOR. — *Aggressive!*

1. *Close friend gone off me — don't know why.* - PASSIVE

2. *Doctor, just not answering my questions at all* -PASSIVE

3. *Being laughed at when I was nervous* AGGRESSIVE - OR THEN SULK & TAKE IT OUT ON PARTNER.

4. *Feeling OK about not knowing everything--in a conversation, for example.* -I PRETEND TO KNOW MORE THAN I DO

5. *Asking for what I want in a sexual relationship.* - PASSIVE, & THEN TALK INDIRECTLY

6. *Saying No to my mother.* PASSIVE, THOUGH I USUALLY DO IT.

7. *Confronting a staff member for B.O.* INDIRECT, TRY TO GET SOMEONE ELSE TO TELL THEM.

8. *Asking for a raise/change in work pattern.* -INDIRECTLY

9. *Being physically used by a man.* PASSIVELY, AS IN A MASSAGE THAT TURNED SEXUAL.

10. *Giving way to anger (Programmed to keep my temper!)* AGGRESSIVE, PASSIVE OR MANIPULATIVE - ANYTHING SO I DONT HAVE TO EXPRESS MY ANGER!

Two more examples of completed lists and assessments

for a while. You may find it useful to look at the examples on pages 15 and 16 which were written by three women who took part in an assertiveness training class. Remember, though, that your own list will be unique.

Exercise 2. When you have the time, look at your list and see if you can range the items in order of difficulty. Look through it and find one which you think is the easiest: one which you can *almost* handle assertively but not quite. Write 'Number 1' next to that on your list. Now find the one which makes you shudder when you think about it – the one which you feel is the most difficult and the most horrifying. This one becomes Number 10. Then take the next easiest one and put Number 2 next to it. Find the next most difficult one and make that Number 9. Continue until you have a range of situations, starting with the easiest one and continuing down to the worst. If you cannot manage to find ten, or if you find that most of your list is bunched together round the top and bottom, do not worry – the important thing is to have a range – some easy ones to start with so that you can gradually work your way down the list.

You will probably be wondering what I mean by 'working down' the list. This brings us to the principal method we use in assertiveness training classes – a method called *role-play*.

Talking and thinking about your behaviour is a start, but of limited value. The way to *change* is to try it out for yourself – and this is how you can do it.

Role-play is borrowed from the traditional techniques of behaviour therapy. It helps the person to rehearse what she wants to say or do in a given situation. Another person takes the complementary role – for example, someone else might sit in for the shopkeeper, the queue jumper, the restaurant manager, the child, husband, friend, parent, boss, and so on – so that the first person can practise handling the situation assertively. Without any learned skill, the person taking the complementary role can identify with the situation and will often surprise herself and everyone else by finding the right words to use, the correct intonation, and many subtle ways of making the role-play situation very real for the person who is practising.

If you doubt the effectiveness of this method, you have only to try it to see how helpful it can be. So many participants initially express great reluctance to try it out, and feel extremely self-conscious at the beginning but after taking part in role-play, they are surprised and convinced of its value. It is not the same as 'play-acting': once you are involved in the role, you find that you feel exactly the same feelings that you do in the real-life situation: anxiety, indignation, guilt, or disappointment. What's more, the person taking the opposite role can be a very helpful source of insight and feedback. There are many tiny details – the tone of your voice, the way you stand, or your eyes, for example – details which you do not notice yourself, but all of which contribute to the overall impression. In this way, someone else can watch and tell you when you are coming across more assertively.

Setting up a role-play situation at home. The other person can be anyone you feel safe with. It is not always advisable to choose one of your family unless you are sure they will take what you are doing seriously and that they understand what you are trying to achieve. For this reason, some women find it easier to practise with a friend, especially if the friend has some understanding of what assertiveness is about.

You may feel a littly silly and self-conscious when you both begin but after a couple of awkward moments you will begin to get absorbed. I know that whenever I have tried something out with a close friend rather than in a class I have always felt a little embarrassment at first but it soon disappears. It is quickly replaced by the excitement of learning with someone's interest and encouragement and the satisfaction is shared by both of you when you finally get it right! Apart from being fun a lot of the time, it is also a very useful and positive way to be a friend to someone.

How do you start? Whether just one of you is practising or both of you intend to take a turn, whoever starts must decide specifically on what they want to achieve. It is no good saying 'I want to cope with unhelpful shopkeepers', 'I want to feel more comfortable talking to my boss' – or 'I want to stop being bullied by my hairdresser'. You have to learn to be specific: 'I want to take back a pair of shoes to the shop and get a replacement', 'I want to ask my boss not to keep giving me work to do last thing on a Friday', or 'I want to tell my hairdresser not to cut more than half an inch off my hair'.

Setting the scene. You do not have to go to too much trouble over this, but it helps to recreate the scene a little. For example, the first role-play might need the person playing the shop assistant to stand behind something which would represent a counter. In the second example the 'boss' might sit at a desk (you could use a table). The boss could pretend to be on the telephone or writing or doing whatever makes the scene more realistic. In the third, the 'hairdresser' could stand behind the other person who could be on a chair, just as you would be in a hairdresser's salon.

You do not have to worry about having dramatic ability. Everyone finds it remarkably easy once they relax into it – we are often better observers of one another's behaviour and gestures than we give ourselves credit for. Remember that the role-play is for the person who is practising the situation. If it is your turn, ask the other person to tell you what you say or do which is unhelpful and work out how you can use what they say to improve the way you handle yourself in that situation.

With practice, you can find out that you need not be afraid of criticism but that someone else's comments can be very revealing and useful. Keep practising again and again until you feel happier with the way you handle the situation.

One word of caution: there is no need whatsoever to feel, once you can manage a problem in a role-play setting, that you should be ready to try it out for real. You may not feel ready for a long time to try it in a real-life setting. This is fine. Recognize that there are alternative ways of coping with a situation. Notice how it *feels* to take an assertive role; see how it feels to identify with a position of confidence rather than anxiety, with a firm and assured stance instead of a defensive one. If you feel ready and want to take the next stage to try out the real thing, then go ahead. But only when *you* feel ready.

Start with the easiest first. The reason for doing this is important. It is tempting to dive into the deep end too soon. The hard problems are the ones you most want to be rid of, the ones which cause you most heartache and frustration. But any long-standing problem usually involves a relationship with someone who is or has been important to you in some way – it may be a person at work, a spouse, a parent or close friend. Any relationship that *matters* to you will have a history attached to it and therefore feelings will run high. It is more difficult to be clear about what you really want and feel when the situation is emotionally loaded. For example, it is almost impossible to say 'no' assertively to your mother when you have been saying 'yes' for thirty years and swallowing back the resentment every time. Long-standing relationships of any kind are fraught with hidden complications. It is no good pretending all you want to do is simply ask your teenage daughter to stop spending hours on the telephone when deep down you are very sad that she is growing away from you. If you start with the Number 9s and 10s, you will probably find that you will get too anxious and that it will not work. Then you will feel discouraged and you will become convinced that there is no way of dealing with it.

Start with situations where you can practise your assertive skills with people who do not mean that much to you – the milkman, the salesman, a neighbour or new work associate or waitress, for example. You can probably find many opportunities which present themselves during your day when you can try out these skills. Nothing is too trivial – every single interaction that you manage assertively will build up your skill and confidence. You can do as little as you want and take as long as you want. You can look at your list as your personal programme. What for you is very easy and would not even appear on your list might be a Number 10 situation for someone else. And, similarly, something which presents you with a lot of difficulty could be easy for someone else to manage. It is not a question of being inferior and superior but of different areas of competence. We can learn a lot from each other, both with helpful comments and support.

As you read through the book you may find more and more situations you would like to try for yourself – you may want to practise an important interview that you know you are going to have to face or you may want to find a better way of handling a recurring problem. The worst hurdle is making a start – it is always easier to *think* about doing it – either before or after the event! Role-play offers the most effective way I know of actually helping people to use the skills for themselves – and to see that they work.

I remember Anna reporting back during the second meeting when I asked if anyone had practised what we had tried out using role-play the week before. Anna, a quiet woman in her early fifties, had said nothing the previous week. But this time, she described how her daughter had bought a shirt which had torn under the arm and that both her daughter and a friend had tried unsuccessfully to get a refund from the store.

On the strength of that initial session, Anna decided to try her assertive skills. In her own words: 'I went in and said, "This shirt is torn and I want my money back." The manager said, "I don't understand, she must have pulled it." "She didn't pull it," I went on, "and I want my money back." "It is not our policy to return money," said the manager. "I don't know anything about that," I replied. "All I know is that I want my money back." And do you know, I got it! As he was giving it to me, he said, "I'm glad we don't have many customers who are such a nuisance," but I didn't care, I felt ten feet tall when I walked out of that shop.' Her whole manner and sense of triumph was applauded spontaneously by the rest of the group.

When Anna said she felt 'ten feet tall', she took a big step forward in building her confidence. If you try to tackle the more difficult problems before you are ready, you will only come unstuck and undo the positive effect of building your self-confidence. On the other hand, with one, two, then three small successes under your belt, you will achieve two things. You will be able to shrug off a failure here and there without too much self-recrimination and despair, and feel better equipped to tackle the more difficult situations from a position of strength. In this way, you will avoid the common barrier which prevents people getting started: the trap of thinking that everything is either too trivial to bother about or too difficult to cope with. A lot of us get stuck in this trap and end up doing nothing. The first and major step is to start applying the actual techniques which are introduced in the next chapter.

4
Techniques

If by now you are interested in knowing how assertive skills can work for you, take a closer look at the dynamics of an ordinary, everyday situation: you are tired, you go home and the place is in an absolute mess – how do you get help with clearing it all up?

What might Agnes do? She runs into the lounge, turns off the television, yanks one of the children by the arm, throws all the toys on the floor, pulls the newspaper out of her husband's hands and yells 'Who the hell do you think you are?'

Dulcie sits at the kitchen table with her head in her hands and then rises and starts to pick up the toys, trudging around thinking to herself, 'They really are so inconsiderate. Look at him sitting there doing nothing. Men have it all their own way.' Then silently, passively, she goes about preparing the meal.

Ivy comes in and mutters, 'Look at this mess! I don't know how you can be so inconsiderate.' She clears the mess and then cooks supper late. If anyone complains about the lateness she responds with a chilling stare. The whole meal is conducted in a heavy, awkward silence and everyone feels uncomfortable and guilty.

Notice that none of them has asked directly for what she wanted – namely some help. This brings us to three skills which are essential to assertive interactions. You need to:

1. Decide what it is you want or feel, and say so specifically and directly.
2. Stick to your statement, repeating it, if necessary, over and over again.

3. Assertively deflect any responses from the other person which might undermine your assertive stance.

Being specific. If you have ever listened to someone's long-winded preamble, you may have wondered impatiently when they were ever going to get to the point. This is the key to this technique. It means deciding what the 'point' is and stating it without all the unnecessary padding that we tend to use when we are anxious. Look at the following examples of padding (in brackets).

'(I hope you don't mind me saying this, you'll probably think I'm very bold, in fact it is unusual for me, but) I do think you look lovely today.'

'(I'm terribly sorry to trouble you but) I'd like you to change this for a clean cup.'

'(Oh, I'd have loved to say "yes" but you know, with things as they are, and, you know, really if you'd told me last week, I mean, you haven't given me much notice, so this time) my answer is "no".'

'(Ahem, waiter, I'm very sorry, but I'm afraid that) my steak is overdone.'

'(I wondered what you were doing this afternoon, you know, if you were busy, because I, em, have to go to the shops, and well, if you're doing anything, I shouldn't really ask, I suppose, but) I'd like to borrow your car.'

The padding often weakens your statement and confuses the listener. Practise making a clear statement or request without the preamble.

It is only when you say what it is you *want* that you can say it with conviction. It is no use, for example, trying to convey assertively that you want to replace a faulty article with another when what you really want is your money back; it is no good trying assertively to arrange where and when to meet someone when your heart is not in it and you really do not want to be going out at all; you will not sound convincing when you ask someone to help you set the table when your real wish was to have been given the evening off, with someone else taking care of the entire meal.

Ask for what you know you want and keep to the point.

Once you have decided on your request or statement, the second hurdle is to be able to say clearly and directly what you want or feel.

Remember that the best chance you have of getting exactly what you want is by asking for it directly and specifically. If you only hint or complain, you will probably hear yourself saying, 'I've asked him *so* many times' or 'I'm always telling her but . . .' Just check whether or not you have made a *clear* request, or if you think the other person *ought* to know what you want and feel, without you having to spell it out for them. We assume that someone should know us well enough by now or that if they loved us enough, they would understand our needs without us having to be explicit. But we cannot always rely on other people's telepathic abilities. Nor is it safe to rely on dropping large hints, however large: uttering a deep sigh and looking heavenwards may still not accurately convey that you want some help with clearing the room. Besides which, if you are not specific, then others can always sidestep the issue conveniently on the grounds that you did not actually ask for anything!

As women we often confuse clarity and directness with bluntness or rudeness. We learn to hint in a roundabout way, to make others feel guilty if they have not responded to our unexpressed needs. We complain, we reproach others, we resort to sarcasm, we sulk. The last thing we do is actually *say* what it is we want. Whether it is the Agnes, the Dulcie or the Ivy which predominates in our behaviour, the problem of identifying the actual need or request poses the same difficulty.

How could you deal with the situation assertively? Selma arrives home and finds the same chaos and mess and her husband sitting in the chair. She confronts him with a statement: 'I'm tired and I'd like you to help me get the supper ready. I would like you to do the washing up (or wash the vegetables or lay the table).' She asks specifically and directly for the help she wants.

Sticking to it. So now you know what you want to say, beginning with an assertive request. But what happens if, as soon as you start, you receive a barrage of abuse or are met with a refusal or even ignored? This is when you move on to the next stage, which is to repeat your statement or request calmly until it is understood and acknowledged by the other person.

The purpose of repetition is to help you maintain a steady position without falling prey to *manipulative comment*, or *irrelevant logic*, or *argumentative bait* – some or all of which will inevitably be provoked by your assertive behaviour. Here are some examples:

In a small supermarket Selma returns some French cheese

which, when opened at home, was revealed to have rather more mould than was healthy!

Selma: I bought this cheese yesterday. When I got home and opened it, I found it was mouldy. I want my money back, please.

Shopkeeper: Nothing to do with me, I wasn't here yesterday. *(Irrelevant logic.)*

Selma: I bought it in this shop and as it is inedible I want my money back, please.

Shopkeeper: That sort of cheese is meant to be mouldy. If you don't like that sort of thing you shouldn't buy it. *(Argumentative bait.)*

Selma: I know what kind of cheese I buy. This is bad and I want my money back.

Shopkeeper: Look, there's a queue of people waiting behind you. Please would you let them pass. It's not fair they should have to wait. *(Manipulative bait.)*

Selma: I can see that there are people behind but I bought this cheese yesterday. It is inedible and I want my money back.

Shopkeeper: Well, how much was it then? *(In a resigned, unfriendly voice, but nevertheless he gives the money back.)*

Selma has an unexpected morning off and intends to spend her time reading. Her next-door neighbour knocks on the door in a fluster.

Neighbour: Selma, dear, what are you doing this morning?

Selma: I'm going to spend it reading.

Neighbour: Oh good. Since you're not busy, would you look after the children while I go to the hairdresser? The only appointment I could get is at 11 o'clock.

Selma: I'm sorry, but I'm not prepared to spend the morning looking after your children.

Neighbour: But Selma, love, what are friends for? *(Manipulative bait.)* You know I like to have my hair done and look nice. I don't often get the chance to go. *(More manipulative bait.)*

Selma: Yes, I know, but I'm still not prepared to look after your children all morning.

Neighbour: *(Sulking.)* It won't be for long, you could read while they played. They wouldn't bother you at all. *(Irrelevant logic.)*

Selma: No, I'm really not prepared to look after your children this morning. Why don't you try someone else? *(The neighbour finally accepts Selma's refusal.)*

Robert, a friend of a distant cousin, landed on Selma's doorstep from Australia. He said he expected to stay a couple of nights but it's now three weeks later. He has spent most of the time watching television, lounging around, helping himself to food and making phone calls.

Selma: Robert, I have something to say to you. I think you have been here quite long enough and I would like you to move on somewhere else.

Robert: Oh come on, Selma, what are you being so heavy about? *(Argumentative bait.)*

Selma: You may think I am being heavy, but you've been here three weeks and I feel that it's now time for you to move on somewhere else.

Robert: How can you chuck me out when I haven't any money? *(Manipulative bait.)*

Selma: You can get yourself a job if you try. You have been here for three weeks and I'd like you to move on somewhere else.

Robert: What am I supposed to do? I'm a stranger here. Look, I'll move next week. Don't worry about it: just calm down and cool it. It really isn't going to make any difference. *(Irrelevant logic.)*

Selma: I am calm, Robert, and I would like you to move somewhere else. *(Robert eventually gets the message.)*

The difficulty with argumentative bait is that as soon as you reply to it, you are hooked and your position is weakened. And remember that in many commercial establishments people are actually trained to deflect customers and to fob them off, or to make it difficult to obtain a refund. After all, their primary concern must be the company's profit margin and not the individual customer's feelings. So this technique works in two ways. First, it helps you to project an image of determination and purpose instead of appearing to be a pushover. Secondly, many women find that after the first two or three repetitions they can actually feel the *truth* of their statement with conviction and are stronger as a consequence – which, of course, reinforces the impression of determination. The technique is remarkably effective, but it does require constant repetition of the key phrase.

Once you are able to repeat your phrase and feel your confidence increase, you then need to cope with the other person's rejoinders. Simply ignoring what they say or pretending you have not heard as you carry on repeating your request is not enough. You will not create an assertive impression sounding like a mechanical parrot with the motor stuck! On the other hand, it is often very difficult not to answer or respond to a red herring in some way. And in doing so, you can become sidetracked and then lose heart. An assertive beginning all too often degenerates into an aggressive outburst or sulky submission, only because of this specific difficulty. This is where the third skill becomes relevant: *fielding responses*.

In order to achieve a smooth verbal interaction and communicate effectively, you need to indicate that you have heard what the other person said, but without getting 'hooked' by what they say. Practising this helps you to overcome your anxiety and defensiveness and to continue undeterred. The following examples show how this might be done.

'It may not be usual for you to get complaints, *but I still want to exchange these goods.*'

'I know there is a queue of people behind me, *but I still want you to exchange these oranges.*'

'I can see you are feeling let down, *but I still don't want to go out tonight.*'

'I can see your other customers aren't complaining, *but this is not what I ordered and I want a replacement.*'

'I know that you need to borrow the typewriter urgently, *but I need it myself right now.*'

'I appreciate you being a good friend to me in the past, *but I am unable to babysit for you tonight.*'

'I know that you're tired as well *but I'd still like you to do your share of the work.*'

'I know you're disappointed, *but I still have to say "no".*'

In each example, the speaker maintains her statement. She acknowledges the response of the other person without getting hooked.

It is extraordinary that these techniques appear so simple. When you come to practise them using role-play, you will probably discover how difficult it can be to stick to your point; how easy it is to be sidetracked; how important it is to decide what you want to say. An approximation will not do – you need to be specific if you want to communicate assertively. Once you become familiar with these basic assertiveness training skills, you will see how often you can apply them to any situation in which you wish to assert yourself more effectively.

Following on

1. If you have made the list of situations as suggested in Chapter 3 you will already have a good idea of where to begin. Look at the situations towards the top of your list. Using the skills outlined above, you can decide what it is you want to say/ask and then try it out in role-play. Sticking to your statement will probably be more difficult than you think but keep going until you feel the conviction of what you are saying. Practise fielding the response from the other person without getting sidetracked.

2. You can practise the techniques with the following sample situations:

a) You have bought a drill and when you get home you find it doesn't work. Set up the role-play with someone to take the part of the shop assistant who implies you don't know how to use the drill because you're a woman, and use the techniques to ask for a replacement.

b) You are sitting in a café. You have asked for a cup of coffee which is brought to you stone cold. Practise asking for a hot cup of coffee in replacement.

c) You want to ask a friend if you can have the book back that you lent them two months ago. The friend has not finished it but you are just about to go away and want to take the book with you to read.

d) You are in a restaurant and the steak you have ordered is tough. You ask for the price of the steak to be deducted from your bill.

e) You see some appealing apples on display in the green-grocer's. You ask for a pound of them but the greengrocer goes to another box of apples, which you suspect are not as good as the others. Your task is to ask for a pound of the apples on display.

f) You want to make an appointment to see a busy supervisor at work. Your task is to use the skills to approach them in the office or in the corridor and get them to agree to a specific time.

g) You are sitting on the bus and someone comes to sit next to you – in fact it feels as if they are sitting on top of you! Practise asking them to move over so you have enough room for yourself.

Use these ideas and adapt them to suit you. There are countless examples of situations in shops, in queues, travelling or eating out which provide excellent opportunities for practising these skills.

5

Our Rights

At this point it is important to consider some basic human rights applicable to all of us, women and men, adults and children. These rights are not new or startling or revolutionary. In fact they may strike some readers as quite ordinary at first, but many women have been helped to make a start in changing their behaviour by reviewing these rights. They have also found it useful to remind themselves of these rights at moments when they felt assailed by doubts and conflict over the rights and wrongs of assertive behaviour.

Experience has taught me that, simple though they sound, it takes a very long time for some of these rights to sink in. It is only after repeated affirmation that we can not only believe them but act on them with conviction.

Eleven rights are set out below, with a brief explanation of each one. Keep them in mind as a reference during the following chapters.

1. *I have the right to state my own needs and set my own priorities as a person independent of any roles that I may assume in my life.* This is fundamental, and particularly so for women, whose roles in life often swamp their own personalities. Women are often referred to as someone's wife or someone's mother. Marriage and motherhood often signal a period in a woman's life when her 'self' goes underground as the demands for child-care and maybe husband-care severely limit any time she has for herself. The responsibilities and

obligations attached to these roles can obstruct the view of what a woman may want for herself, rather than what she feels she *should* want as a mother or wife or daughter.

I remember Carol's sense of triumph when she made a decision to go on holiday alone. Her husband wanted her to go with him and Carol felt obliged because she had previously spent two holidays with her mother. Her mother wanted her back and Carol felt torn because she was the only daughter. The conflict between these two roles had lasted several months while Carol fretted and postponed making a decision. In the class where the emphasis was placed repeatedly on what *she* wanted to do, she suddenly saw quite clearly that she really wanted to go away on her own. When she made this announcement assertively to both her husband and her mother, to her amazement, they both accepted her decision quite easily.

This right does not imply that you no longer have to honour the responsibilities within the roles you assume. It simply helps you to be aware that your own needs exist as well as the needs of those for whom you care.

Julie, a hard-working health visitor, had great difficulty in setting aside time for herself and felt that her patients should always have priority. So she was always available and fulfilled her role admirably except that her own needs were submerged and went unrecognized. They did not disappear though – her unspoken needs emerged in her perpetual tiredness and tension.

Making time for yourself can be an important new step. For as long as Elizabeth could remember she had wanted to learn another language. But, busy with a household of three teenage children, she had never been able to find the time. The combination of a recent holiday in Spain and an information brochure sent through the post from the local evening institute pushed her to a decision to attend an evening class in Spanish. When she settled down to do her fifteen minutes' homework practice in the evening, she was met with a barrage of comments from her family, such as 'What do you want to learn Spanish for at your age?' mixed with the usual requests for clean shirts and lost books! It was difficult for her, but Elizabeth managed to make that time for *herself* a priority. It can be easy for a woman to feel that because she is a woman, because she is a mother or a wife, she should not have certain feelings or personal needs. It can be difficult to assert those needs and individual wants when they conflict with the role.

2. *I have the right to be treated with respect as an intelligent, capable and equal human being.* On a good day, this is an easy one

to accept, but one of the difficulties is that we often do not treat *ourselves* with respect. We do not give ourselves equal credit for intelligence or ability. Intelligence is a quality that many women have consciously played down in order to retain a suitably feminine image. Others who feel comfortable in asserting their intelligence can lose sight of it when faced with a situation in which they feel disadvantaged by lack of technical expertise. You may know, for instance, that your brakes do not work any more effectively after paying for a service on your car than before. You confront the garage mechanic or manager who rattles off all sorts of explanations that you suspect are flannel. It is easy to feel confused in this sort of confrontation and it is important to hold on to the fact that you *know* that your brakes are not working, rather than being pushed against the wall by the force of an argument which has you doubting your own intelligence and common sense.

3. *I have the right to express my feelings.* One of the most important lessons in assertiveness training is learning to recognize what you are feeling *at the time*. Often we agonize over an event hours, days, or even months later before we finally register what it was we felt. It is important to identify and to accept what you feel and permit yourself some verbal expression. (As we will discuss later, in Chapter 9, there is a difference between the *expression* of what you feel and acting on it.) Accepting the truth of what you feel can serve as an antidote to the cultural declamation of feelings. You can express your feelings without fearing the accusations of being 'hysterical' or 'irrational'. You can express the negative and positive feelings instead of holding back. Many people have lost touch with their emotions and consequently the validity of emotional expression has been diminished. This right has three aspects – recognizing and identifying your feelings, accepting rather than denying them and then choosing to express them appropriately.

4. *I have the right to express my opinions and values.* This includes the right to stand up for your opinions if you choose. This is not to say that you should be bullied into justifying an opinion or particular viewpoint if you do not want to, but it means that you have the right to your own opinions even if they stand in dis-agreement with those of the majority. It is not a question of right or wrong – but of differences in perception.

Sometimes we lose sight of our right to assert our own values. I remember Michelle, who collected pieces of china, agonizing over a friend who treated these objects around her flat with a careless disregard for their fragility and value. She would watch him in silent apprehension as he mishandled and actually damaged pieces that were important to her. I asked her why she did not confront him. She replied that she felt she had no right to be what she described as 'materialistic'. 'It shouldn't matter to me,' she said. 'I shouldn't mind about *things.'* So she reproached herself and felt that her friend's more casual attitude stemmed from a more acceptable philosophy. She denied her own values and simply rationalized her feelings, but inside she continued to carry a grudge. It took a long time for her to acknowledge openly that she *did* feel resentful. Eventually she was able to give herself permission to follow through with those feelings, to consider that her own values were different but equal to and as important as those of her friend. She was able to ask him assertively to treat her objects with the care that *she* felt appropriate.

5. *I have the right to say 'yes' or 'no' for myself.* This sounds simple but is very much connected with the first right about roles and responsibilities. Making a choice for yourself because *you* want or do not want something becomes more difficult when you have other roles to fulfil.

I was struck by Doreen's comment about what assertiveness had meant for her; she described a conversation with her son who was questioning her about a course she applied for. When he asked her why she was doing this particular course, she found herself, as usual, about to justify her choice on the grounds of convenience and economy when she stopped and replied quite simply: 'Because I want to.' She told the group that previously she had not felt that she was important enough to give that kind of response, but now she felt that it was enough just to say that she wanted it. No further justification was necessary.

6. *I have the right to make mistakes.* Many of us find it extraordinarily difficult to accept this right. If someone points out a mistake or criticizes an action, we are often covered with shame and confusion out of all proportion to the seriousness of the actual error. Whether it is the experience of being punished as children for mistakes, or the whole educational construct – of right and wrong, of good marks and bad marks – I am not sure; but many of us believe that making a mistake is unacceptable and that it shows we are stupid.

You can learn to shrug your shoulders and accept your mistakes without disappearing into a pit of self-reproach or defensively denying your error. A lot us us set store by competence and achievement, and in a competitive society it is difficult to create options other than 'I'm right' and 'you're wrong' or 'I'm wrong' and 'you're right'. It is important to see that you can *do* something stupid without it implying that in essence you *are* stupid or unintelligent. You can behave incorrectly, make a wrong move or do a bad job without it indicating some intrinsic flaw in your character. This right can permit us to acknowledge the mistaken piece of behaviour without losing that central core of self-belief.

7. *I have the right to change my mind.* This right can be invaluable during the early stages of learning to make assertive choices, that is, choices which reflect what you *want* rather than what you feel is expected of you or what you think would suit the other person. As you look more carefully at the process of decision-making you will develop an awareness of how you make many decisions for the wrong reasons. A wrong decision brings regret. You then have to try to back out in some way. There is usually a period of practice needed before being able to make the right decision in starting, and at least while you are learning, you can assertively change your mind rather than proceed with a commitment you are unhappy about.

8. *I have the right to say I don't understand.* Have you ever experienced being in a group of people, with everyone listening in attentive comprehension to the speaker while you sat confused and uncomfortable because you did not understand but felt unable to speak up and admit it, or to ask for another explanation? If so, then you will recognize the importance of this right. As with the right to make mistakes, we do feel an undue amount of shame as adults in acknowledging lack of comprehension and ignorance. We can hardly expect to know everything about everything any more than we can expect to be perfect. But to say 'I don't understand' or 'Could you explain that again?' remains difficult for many of us.

It is so simple to ask, but we hold back time and time again. With this right in mind you can learn to acknowledge confusion or non-comprehension without feeling stupid. You can learn to ask for more information or a repeated explanation without feeling ridiculous.

9. *I have the right to ask for what I want.* Again, this sounds quite straightforward. No one would argue with you. Until, that is, it conflicts with their wishes or expectations. Then accusations of making a fuss or causing upset to a loved-one follow. A direct request is something which many women avoid. They feel they risk refusal with a direct approach. Subtle hints and suggestions are much safer. It is easier to sigh with tiredness and complain of a

backache than to ask someone directly to bring in the washing or move a heavy table.

Many women just go along with what someone else wants for the sake of peace and quiet. I recently heard a good example of this. At the table next to mine in a restaurant sat a man, his wife, their teenage daughter and the grandmother who was visiting the family. The proximity of our tables and my insatiable fascination with other people's conversations allowed me to overhear the following dialogue.

Husband (as they all sit perusing the menu):   Now Mother, what would you like?
Mother: I think I'll have the Chicken Madras.
Husband (in disbelief):   Chicken Madras? Have you ever tasted a Madras? It will be far too hot for you!
Mother (a little hesitantly):   But I *like* it hot.
Husband: Yes, but you don't know what you are talking about. A Madras is the hottest curry you can get.
Mother: But I *like* it hot.
Wife: It really is very hot you know, are you sure?
Grandchild: It really is hot, Gran.
Grandmother: Well . . .
Husband: Look, Mother, if you insist then I will order you a Madras, but don't blame me when you can't eat it.
Waiter arrives to take the order.
Husband: Well Mother, you've decided on the Madras curry, then, have you?
Mother: Emm, I think I'll have a Chicken Korma. Is that mild?

The rest of the family sat back in satisfaction, feeling that she had made the right choice. Maybe the Madras would have been too hot, but I'll never know. What was important for me was that she just gave in. Many women spend their lives going along with what others want and what other people tell them they want. We settle for things we do not want, for something that is not *quite* right because we do not feel we have the right to persist. It is useful to remind yourself of this right over and over again.

10. *I have the right to decline responsibility for other people's problems.* 'But isn't that unkind, selfish, uncaring?' women ask. The right to decline responsibility does not imply that we should not *choose* to put other people first. The trouble is that many women feel that everyone else's problems are their concern. If someone

is unhappy, in trouble, penniless, out of work, inadequate or depressed, they have to take on the responsibility. The problem arises not in choosing to care for those we love but in *compulsively* taking care of everyone else all of the time so that there is no time or consideration for our own personal needs. Choosing to care for another is different from being manipulated into doing so by emotional blackmail. Despite our better judgement, we are often worn down by persistent hard-luck stories or pleas of poverty, misfortune or overwork. Under pressure, we give in to all sorts of demands which force us to accommodate the needs of others, rather than setting limits for ourselves. This right involves setting our own limits about who to care for and whose needs to put before our own. Deciding where to draw the line is what is important.

11. *I have the right to deal with others without being dependent on them for approval.* This final right is one which I think forms a baseline for all of the others. The need for approval is the single most important factor in the realms of unassertive behaviour and it is buried very deep in most of us. It seems to be endemic in our traditional upbringing of both male and female children that appropriate behaviour is rewarded with 'There's a good girl' or 'Daddy's very pleased with you'. An early association is thus instilled between behaving in a way which is approved of and the likelihood of earning a loving response. Although this early learning applies to both boys and girls, various theories show that girls' experience enforces this need to be good, smiling, attractive and feminine in order to gain the desired approbation.

The result of this is that many adult women still fear disapproval because it threatens the very roots of their self-esteem. This is what holds so many women back from stating their needs, expressing their feelings, standing up for their rights, refusing to do something they do not want to because they cannot tolerate the other person's anticipated disapproval. 'What will they think of me if I say no?', 'If I don't apologize?', 'If I express my resentment?', 'If I say I don't want to or that I don't like that?' 'What will they think of me?' is the stumbling block at which many assertive intentions founder.

This need to be liked and approved of is so powerful that it extends way beyond intimates and friends, whose opinions we feel *do* matter and are important to us. It extends to the greengrocer selling rotten vegetables, which you do not like to point out in case he thinks you are a trouble-maker; to the waiter who might think you are being a nuisance if you ask for something out of the ordinary; to the people in the queue who might think you are aggressive and loud if you complain to the person who has just barged in front of you; to the money collector at the door who will think you are mean if you do not give to the needy children of the parish.

Remember that most of the time, although we project this disapproval on to others, it is only symptomatic of the internal critic which we will look at again in the chapter on self-esteem. The more effectively you can silence, or at least reduce, your own internal critic to realistic proportions, the more successfully you can assess your own behaviour and unhook yourself from dependence on the opinion of others.

This dependence and need for approval is crippling, and it takes courage to shake it. After a few experiences of surviving someone's disapproval and the realization that the world did not come to an end, it becomes easier. You can also feel proud at having handled a situation assertively and boosted your *own* morale independently. You can learn that you can actually get by without the approval and acceptance of everybody all of the time!

Early on in an assertiveness training class, participants are asked to consider these basic rights. The list looks simple at first and includes rights that sometimes seem too obvious to be spelt out at all – for example, the right to be treated as an equal human being. Other rights prove more difficult to accept, such as the right to decline responsibility for other people's problems. It usually takes a while for these rights to make an impression. It is one thing to accept them at an intellectual level, but it takes time to understand their full significance.

Take, for example, the right to make a mistake. You know that you accept that right, but what happens to your convictions when someone is actually criticizing a mistake in your work? Or when your cake flops? Or somebody points out that you have just contradicted yourself? Or the curtains that you have chosen for your room are really disastrous? If you feel overwhelmed with confusion, you will recognize that at stressful times, we often forget these rights. It is here that assertiveness training can help: learning to respond assertively when you are under fire; learning to hold on to the knowledge of your basic rights when you need them most; learning to operate from a base of inner certainty and self-esteem.

6

Body Language

The assertive woman, as we have seen, needs to speak out firmly and clearly. But 'speaking out' involves much more than the words you use. Your entire body helps you to assert yourself. Your posture, your expression, your gestures will create a total impression. Non-verbal messages either reinforce or cancel out what you are trying to convey verbally. This chapter is concerned with how to use your body to convey an assertive presence.

An attempt to manage a situation assertively may fail, even though your words are exactly right, because your tone of voice and posture or facial expression show uncertainty or self-doubt or hostility.

Fortunately, you do not have to adopt a whole new set of gestures or expressions to learn assertive body language. That would only make you appear affected and self-conscious. Body language emerges spontaneously from your feelings at the moment. *Feeling* assertive is the first step towards exuding assertiveness with your *entire* body.

But there are body patterns that we can *unlearn*. As women, for example, most of us have learned how to smile appealingly, to gesture coyly, to pout, to wheedle and coax with our entire bodies. These habits get in the way of assertive communication. If you take the time to observe how you use your own body, you will see how you can come across more effectively.

1. Posture. The first thing to consider is your posture – the way you hold yourself says a lot about you. Notice whether you hold yourself upright or slouched; whether your shoulders are hunched up around your ears (we often do this when anxious) or are down in a relaxed position. If you are standing or sitting, notice whether you are balanced or leaning on one leg or buttock. It is impossible to be assertive standing off-balance! Notice how you walk into a room. Do you shuffle in, hoping not to be noticed, march in like a thunderbolt, or move steadily holding your head up and your back straight? Notice whether your head is upright or cocked to one side.

The relative height between you and the other person is another factor. I remember Sylvia reporting that on a particular occasion, she was facing a man sitting at a big desk which towered over her as she sank into the low armchair in front of it. She was negotiating a contract so she needed all the confidence she could muster. She suddenly realized how disadvantaged she felt in that position, so she slowly rose and walked to a radiator at the wall against which she leant so that she could be just a little higher yet not tower over him. That small move increased her assurance and she negotiated more equally and successfully.

2. Proximity/distance. Each of us responds to an invisible line between ourselves and another person: too far back from it, the other person feels inaccessible and you feel ineffectual; too far over that line and you feel too close. An important learning point is that we often have differing optimum distances: so that what is too close for you may well be comfortable for another and, conversely, someone else may be most comfortable with a distance which feels to you as if you have lost contact altogether. Learn what is an effective distance for you.

Gillian's problem provides an illustration. She complained that when she wanted to approach her boss she would knock and enter his office. Her boss sat behind the desk and would often not even look up. She would be told to come back later, talked at through a telephone conversation or completely ignored. When we re-enacted this situation in role-play in the class, Gillian found that her entry into the room and the proximity to the desk made all the difference. Pausing to breathe outside and get herself into an assertive frame of mind, she entered more calmly. Then she moved just two feet nearer the desk and stood squarely in front of her boss.

Notice how you approach someone. Do you sidle up and stand at an angle or do you walk straight up and stand in front? You have more chance of conveying a direct approach, if you stand or sit directly in front of the other person.

FACIAL EXPRESSION

'Pleased to meet you'   'I feel confident'   'Leave me alone...'

'I'm being serious...'   'I'd love to do it'   'I'm angry with you'

POSTURE

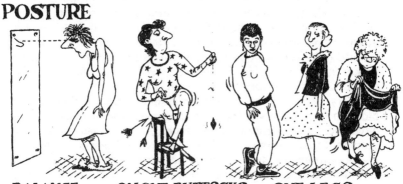

BALANCE · · · ON ONE BUTTOCK? ~ ONE LEG?

3. Eyes. When we describe the eyes as the 'windows of the soul', we indicate their obvious power of communication. We feel uneasy about shifty gazes, and disconcerted when we cannot see the reactions in someone's eyes – as when they are wearing totally opaque or reflective sunglasses. Unconsciously we look for a reaction most of the time. The eyes tell us whether someone is listening or not; whether they are impressed, fascinated or intimidated by what we are saying. It is infuriating to try and talk to someone who has their back to you or has their attention focused on the television. It is also difficult to talk to someone when they look at you very directly without ever shifting their gaze – you feel stared at and the gaze feels intrusive. Somewere in between is the 'normal' interaction. Your gaze can be relaxed and friendly or it can convey hostility and timidity. If you avert your eyes, you probably convey embarrassment. Being able to look directly at someone while making an assertive request or statement can greatly reinforce the message.

4. Mouth and jaw. Moving down to the lower part of your face, we find other subtle signals: a clenched jaw or a tightly-held mouth are give-away signs, which communicate tension and aggression. In role-play, assertion slips easily into aggression when, although the words the speaker uses are exactly the same, her jaw tightens and her chin juts forward slightly. As soon as that happens – maybe with a slight thrust forward of the shoulders – the atmosphere changes because the body language is seen as threatening and hostile.

In psychological jargon a give-away signal is known as 'non-verbal leakage'. This describes the cues that do not quite fit, the clues which give away the real feelings of the speaker despite her attempt to control and disguise them. One example is the smile that is a little too fixed or too wide or which lasts too long. Such a smile makes us uncomfortable because we detect there is something false about it. This does not necessarily imply that the person is deliberately trying to deceive the listener. Sometimes we feel obliged to hide our hurt or embarrassment or anger because we feel we do not have the right to express those feelings or because we feel too vulnerable and unsafe. Similarly, we try to disguise our fury or disappointment because we are afraid we might blow up in a temper or burst into tears – neither of which are considered socially acceptable.

When it comes to expressing anger, most women will make angry statements while smiling unawares at the same time. This is

certainly not because they are feeling happy or friendly at that precise moment! It is usually because of the nervousness and inhibition they feel about expressing anger. The automatic smile is really a non-verbal message saying 'Please don't be angry with me' or 'I don't want to appear nasty'!

Many of us have been so conditioned to be 'nice' that this smile is a vestige of that niceness, of that encouragement to be sweet, appealing and placating. Similarly, when women practise making a statement expressing hurt or resentment, an inappropriate smile creeps across the face. If you are saying that you are angry or hurt with a broad smile on your face, it is bound to confuse the other person and detract from the force of your statement. The two elements do not match up. And you are left wondering why people do not take you seriously!

5. Voice. If you have ever experienced irritation at being in the company of someone who continually speaks in a very loud voice, or been frustrated by always having to lean forward and say, 'pardon?' to someone who talks in a scarcely audible whisper, you will understand the difference the volume of your voice can make. Between the 'little girl' voice and the foghorn, there is a balance. Practise using the higher and lower registers of your voice. Breathing and relaxation help release the constriction of the throat and chest to use a deeper breath to project your voice more fully.

The difference between an assertive and aggressive interaction is often conveyed in these subtle changes in the pitch and tone of the voice. Notice whether your voice is a whine or whether it carries an apologetic or sarcastic or hostile tone. Speaking more slowly and audibly instead of mumbling or muttering some garbled statement will ensure clearer comprehension. The inflection of your voice is also important. If you are making an assertive statement, do not let your voice rise up at the end, making your statement sound like a question. You can say any word with conviction or half-heartedly. An edge to your voice can make a refusal sound like a put-down instead of a firm but non-aggressive statement.

6. Gestures. Twiddling a piece of hair, scratching the scalp, clasping and unclasping the hands, or biting your fingers or the side of your mouth, fiddling with jewellery, all these gestures convey tension and nervousness. Tapping or shuffling feet send out messages of impatience and embarrassment. 'Chopping' movements of hands and arms can express anger.

Once you are aware of your gestures, you can learn to keep them under control. The experience of role-playing provides an opportunity to observe and comment. This is both illuminating and helpful. Sometimes only slight readjustments are necessary: refraining from twiddling, standing up straighter, breathing three times calmly before approaching a difficult confrontation, sitting or standing in a well-balanced position, altering the tone of your voice, holding your arms by the side instead of clasped together anxiously behind your back, your shoulders relaxed instead of hunched around your ears. These minor alterations can make an enormous difference to how you *feel* and as a consequence to how you present yourself.

7. Appearance. One final aspect of non-verbal communication is appearance. Drawing your attention to appearance is *not* to urge you to conform to any convention of dress for the purpose of attracting an onlooker. It is much more to do with how you feel about *yourself* – our appearance says a lot about our mood and how we feel about our bodies; the colours we wear, the parts of our bodies we choose to emphasize or conceal; the sorts of clothes we choose.

Feeling assertive can have the effect of making you want to express yourself clearly in your appearance. Many class members have begun to make little changes, to do something different, not out of a need to impress but out of a new-found wish to express their own personality. Finding a personal style, discovering something which expresses *you* does not need a lot of money or time – just a belief that you are worth knowing and caring about.

You can see that every one of these individual features contributes to the total impression. The way to start changing the overall effect is to focus on the detail. Most of us are quite unaware of a facial expression or simple gesture which is immediately obvious to an observer so the best way to learn is by asking someone else to comment. Use their eyes to see where you go wrong. Improve your body language and you will find that with only minor adjustments, you will be able to produce a major change in the general effectiveness of your communication and self-presentation.

7
Saying 'No'

When a woman says 'no', she really means 'yes' . . . or so the saying goes. Many women feel a sense of outrage at its preposterous implications. But the fact is that women find it difficult to say 'no' clearly and definitely. So when we do say 'no', we say so indirectly and without conviction. Learning how to make an assertive refusal – with clarity, persistence and without aggression – is what this chapter is about.

Consider some of the situations in which it is difficult for you to make a refusal: a request for money; a social invitation; a loan, or a lift, or some information that you don't want to give. Who do you find most difficult to refuse? A stranger at the door, your partner, a child, an old person, your boss, your mother? When do you find it difficult? When you are tired, in a rush, in front of a group of people, on the telephone?

Although the type of difficulty will vary from person to person, there are common beliefs which come up time and time again. These are some of the most common:

Saying 'no' is callous, uncaring and mean. It's selfish.

Saying 'no' over little things shows you're churlish, small-minded or petty.

Saying 'no' directly is rude and aggressive. It's too abrupt and blunt.

Saying 'no' will cause others to take offence. It will make them feel hurt and rejected.

If you believe any or all of these myths, you will probably find you have difficulty in making clean, clear statements of refusal. Do you find yourself falling into any of the following traps, like Ivy? Padding out a refusal with a load of excuses, including dishonest ones, such as: 'It doesn't belong to me, otherwise I'd love to lend it to you . . .' 'He's not very well, otherwise I'd love to come . . .' 'My mother wouldn't like it!' Or have you ever tried to avoid saying 'no' directly by making the other person feel guilty: 'I don't know how you could ask that of me when you can see what I've been going through . . .?' Have you ever tried to soften the blow with a winning smile or a patronizing manner which you hope will convince everyone you are not just being nasty? Excuses, avoidance and pussy-footing have become entrenched habits.

We have acquired accompanying body habits as well. The most noticeable one is the inappropriate smile which we discussed earlier. The more we try to cover our anxiety about saying 'no' with an appearance of graciousness, the more often our smile and whole body stance come across as ingratiating. What is more, it is often confusing for the other person, who is hearing and watching you say 'no' but with a tone of voice, gestures and manner of someone saying 'yes'. Small wonder that messages get muddled.

The anxiety we feel when saying 'no' leads to another habit. Instead of refusing a request and moving away, it has the effect of keeping our feet rooted to the spot. After a clean, decisive 'no', it would often be more appropriate to leave; but we hover and dither, thus reducing the effectiveness of our refusal and offering the other person an opportunity to put pressure on us to change our minds.

So there are some new habits to be acquired. Someone approaches you and asks you a favour. What happens inside you? What is the very first thing you feel? This is the first step:

Notice your immediate reaction. As soon as someone asks something of you, your body will let you know how you feel about the request, often before you have opened your mouth to reply.

The feelings can be easy to identify when they are very clear. If you want to respond with wholehearted enthusiasm, you may feel like jumping at the opportunity – you will be certain you want to say.'yes'. At the other extreme, you can experience a sinking feeling which indicates reluctance, that you definitely want to say 'no'.

The difficulty occurs when the feelings are not so apparent –when you are confused, uncertain, uneasy, doubtful about how you want to respond. Your body will still give you an immediate indication of what you are feeling – if you listen for it. But sometimes we need to learn to listen for that inner guide!

Many women fall into the unfortunate habit of ignoring that immediate guide. Instead of recognizing it and following through, they dismiss it, because of the pressure of what is expected, what is wanted, and what will please. They attend more to the outward impression than the internal need.

It happens so quickly! But you know what happens: you agree or half agree, and then, hours or even days later, you are agonizing about how to get out of a situation or kicking yourself for saying 'yes' when you wanted to say 'no'.

So the first step is to watch for the guide. Never ignore it. If it is a definite 'yes' or 'no' then you can say so. If you find yourself hesitating, even slightly, try the next step.

Try saying 'I don't know. I need some more information.' Do not be pushed. You do not have to be ready to make an instant decision. Acknowledge your uncertainty and confusion and give yourself time by asking for more information. This helps in two ways: it can act as an invaluable mental breathing space which gives you enough time to think for yourself. A simple phrase, such as 'I need to think about it' gives you time to unhook yourself from the automatic pattern of answering *before* you think. You may need no more than a few moments to identify what it is you want to say. Or you may need several days, depending on the circumstances. Take as long as you need, but remember your first reaction is often an infallible guide as to how you honestly want to respond.

The second way this helps is by giving you the information which may genuinely be relevant to how you decide. For example: 'How long do you want me to babysit?', 'When could I expect the money back?', 'Are you really just inviting me to dinner?', 'If I were to take on this position what would be my responsibilities?' You may provoke a surprised reaction in the other person. People often get defensive, especially if their intentions are not really honourable or if they are expecting you to say 'yes' automatically. It forces them to be straight and clear themselves in making a request, which not everyone welcomes. A lot of people prefer to shuffle about in the half light of inexplicit statements and assumptions in which they can hide away from responsibility. But have courage in persisting if it is important to you.

It may be helpful at this juncture to remember the right to change your mind. It can act as a half-way house while you are still learning to say 'no' on the spot. We have become so unaccustomed to thinking for ourselves, to knowing what we want, that an assertive and immediate refusal takes a lot of practice. So a commendable compromise which many women have found helpful is the following: you do not have to suffer for an unassertive decision. If you realize that you really wanted to say 'no', do not avoid answering the phone or waste time concocting all sorts of acceptable excuses. Try taking the situation into your own hands, and communicating your change of heart in a firm and assertive manner.

This brings us to the actual practice of saying 'no'.

Practise saying 'no' without excessive apology or excuses. There is a difference between an explanation and excuses. Ask yourself whether you are explaining because of your own anxiety or because you genuinely want the other person to understand your reasons. Are you genuinely sorry not to be able to help? Are you *really* disappointed not to be able to accept an invitation? It is not always helpful to embellish a refusal with all sorts of gratuitous protestations of regret.

Also practise saying the word 'no'. Many women find it surprisingly difficult to force the word through their reluctant lips! Saying 'no' 'nicely' usually means not saying it at all. If you are one of those people who think, mistakenly, that you will spare someone else's feelings by letting them down gently, then consider who you are really protecting. Much of the indirectness that muddies an assertive refusal is a way of avoiding a clear acknowledgement of responsibility. It can simply be a way of saying 'Please don't dislike me', or 'It's not my fault' or 'Don't be cross with me for saying "no".'

If you have ever felt embarrassed and uncomfortable at the receiving end of one of those long-winded refusals, all plumped up with excuses and nonsense, you will appreciate the value of a plain, straightforward 'no'. At least you know where you stand.

When making a refusal, try accepting responsibility for doing so. You do not need to blame someone else or pass the buck. Changing 'I can't' to 'I don't want to'; changing 'They wouldn't like' to 'I don't like' are simple yet surprisingly effective.

The predominant feature of the problems encountered in assertive refusals is the feeling of guilt. It seems that we are riddled with guilt which comes from every direction. We will look more closely at some of the sources in the next chapter, but for now consider the following maxim: *When you say 'no', you are refusing the request, not rejecting the person.*

Please read the above statement again. You will probably find that it will require a major psychological readjustment. We have come to associate a refusal with rejection, so that it is almost impossible not to see them as synonymous. This is not to say that a refusal will never be felt as rejection or that you have not felt rejected when someone said 'no' to you. But refusal does not *need* to be a rejection. A lot depends on the way you refuse. For example:

1. Jenny and Sheila have been friends for a couple of years. They were colleagues in the same office until Jenny left but they still keep in touch and have lunch together quite often. On this particular occasion, Jenny tells Sheila that she is just off to book a week's package holiday in Spain – a short winter break. Sheila immediately jumps at the idea and proposes that since she also has a week's leave to take, she could go with her to Spain. Jenny does not know how to respond. Her immediate feeling is uncertainty – they are friends but she is not sure whether they could successfully go on holiday together and anyway she is actually looking forward to going away on her own.

How can she handle this situation? She can say 'yes' and then pull out later. She can put aside her fears and tell herself that it will probably be all right and then risk ruining her week away. Or she can make an assertive refusal as follows:

Jenny: I feel quite awkward saying this, Sheila, but I don't think it would be a good idea.
Sheila: Why on earth not? We both like sitting in the sun and lazing around, don't we?
Jenny: Yes, that's true but I must say no because I do actually want to go away on my own.
Sheila: I don't understand you. It seems a very good idea to me.
Jenny: Look Sheila, I value our friendship very much. I enjoy meeting and talking to you but I just don't feel ready to go on holiday with you and I have planned to go away on my own. That is what I want to do.
Sheila: Well, I'm sorry I asked.
Jenny: Don't apologize. Do you feel I've rejected you now?
Sheila: Well, I feel a bit upset but I guess it's best for you to make the right decision now. It would be awful to go away and then find you'd rather be on your own.
Jenny: Thank you for understanding. I do value our time together – but I know this is the right decision.

2. Maggie is dreading going home this Christmas. She knows her mother expects her to stay there for the holiday period as usual but she really doesn't want to go. She wants to spend the time on her own, seeing her friends at home. But as she isn't married with a family, her mother finds it impossible to understand what reason Maggie could have for not going home.

Maggie telephones rather than waiting for the inevitable phone call from her mother.

Maggie: Hello, Mum.

Mother: Hello, dear. We were wondering when we'd hear from you. We're looking forward to seeing you up here soon. When will you be arriving?

Maggie: Well, Mum. That's what I was phoning about. I've decided that I am going to spend Christmas on my own at home.

Mother: You can't spend Christmas on your *own.*

Maggie: Yes, I can, Mum. That's what I want to do.

Mother: But your Dad and I have been so looking forward to it. It won't be the same. . .

Maggie: I know that, but I want to spend Christmas in my own home.

Mother: It will be very miserable for us without you. I mean, I know there's nothing much for you to do but I thought you always liked it here.

Maggie: I do like seeing you but I really don't want to come up for Christmas.

Mother: Oh, well. Your Dad'll be upset, though.

Maggie: I know he will and I know you are too, Mum. Try and understand that it's not you I am rejecting. I love you both very much and want to come and spend time with you but I do want to spend this Christmas on my own here.

Mother: Well, I don't understand but still. You're a grown woman now, I suppose you've got to lead your own life.

Maggie: Thanks, Mum. Having said that, I would like to come and see you over the New Year weekend. Would that be all right?

3. Sally has met Ian at a party. At the time, she enjoyed talking with him, so she agreed to his proposal to meet for a drink during the week. When they meet and spend the evening together, Sally realizes that they really have very little in common and that she isn't interested in spending more time with him. During the course of the evening her discomfort steadily grows as she

realizes that he is feeling very much more attracted to her than she is to him and that he obviously wants to extend and deepen the relationship. She knows she doesn't really want this. She could agree to see him again, knowing that she would pull out later or she could state her decision clearly there and then. How can she do that without rejecting him and hurting his feelings? As they are about to leave, Ian asks if she wants to go to the cinema the following week:

Sally: Ian, this is very difficult to say but I really don't think it would be a good idea for us to meet again.

Ian: Why not? I didn't think you had anyone else?

Sally: I don't have anyone else, that's true, but I would rather be clear now than risk being dishonest and more hurtful later. I have enjoyed our two evenings together but I don't want to make another date.

Ian: You certainly know how to hit below the belt, don't you?

Sally: I'm not hitting below the belt, but I know that it must sound very abrupt and hurtful to you. It's just that my experience has taught me that if I don't make a clear decision at the start, then everything gets very messy.

Ian: But your feelings might change.

Sally: Well, they might but right now that's how I feel.

Ian: Well, there's not much more to say, is there?

Sally: No, I suppose there isn't. Thank you for an enjoyable evening.

4. For the second year running Monica has been invited to give a series of lectures in Manchester. Last year, she wrote to her longstanding friend, Penny, saying that she was coming and Penny was delighted to offer her a room in her house. Although Monica was happy to spend time with Penny, she found the household of four children a little too boisterous. She found it difficult to prepare her work because of constant interruptions and the general mayhem of a large family atmosphere conflicted with her need for tranquillity and solitude. She has just received a letter from Penny inviting her to stay again this year. Monica is unsure how to tell Penny that she wants to stay in a hotel. She could just avoid telling her and then hope she doesn't bump into her. She can 'take care' of her friend's feelings and stay in her house, denying her need for privacy. Or she can explain assertively. She telephones Penny:

Monica: Penny, it's very kind of you to offer me hospitality again but I have decided to take a room in a hotel this time.

Penny: But why go to all that expense when you can stay here free?

Monica: I know it would be cheaper to stay with you, but I need some peace and quiet to prepare my work and I think an anonymous hotel room would be better.

Penny: But the twins are very happy to move out of their room for you. They've been excited about your visit for weeks.

Monica: That's very kind, but I really do want to stay in a hotel.

Penny: I feel terrible. You should have said last time if they were bothering you.

Monica: They weren't bothering me, Penny. You were very kind and hospitable. It's just that I need to get away from everything at the end of the seminar each day and it's easier to stay in a hotel.

Penny: Well, we'll be sorry not to see you.

Monica: I'll be sorry too but I know it's the best decision for me. There is one thing though. I should like to see you all while I'm there. Could I come round for a meal one evening? Would that be convenient?

There are some useful guidelines to keep in mind when making an assertive refusal which can potentially feel like rejection to the other person.

Equality. A refusal does not have to be heavy, aggressive or hurtful. By clearly taking responsibility for your decision, you can also give the other person equal space to express their feelings. This allows the other person to feel acknowledged even though you are saying 'no'. They do not feel their needs have simply been overridden or ignored. This equality is also reflected in the importance of not doing something for someone just because you feel sorry for them. Submerging your own needs when you want to refuse is not necessarily charitable. It can also be invalidating and demeaning for the other person. Think twice before acting out of pity.

Do not hang around. One practical point is not to hover around after a refusal. This only confuses the issue and encourages the other person to try and get you to change your mind. Our anxiety at refusing often keeps us immobile – so we stand there rooted to the spot or stay on the phone when it would be much better to leave or put the phone down. Sometimes, it is appropriate to offer a compromise. Maggie and Monica offered a compromise which felt right because it did not negate what they had decided. On the other hand, Sally needed to leave the matter and go because there was no point in drawing it out any longer. It is important to follow through on your refusal. Backtracking weakens your position and confuses everyone concerned. If you stand firm, people know exactly where they are with you.

Acknowledge your feelings. Both Jenny and Sally began by acknowledging the awkwardness they were experiencing. A simple statement 'I feel guilty' or 'I find this difficult' allows you to express your feelings honestly. If you try and disguise your feelings, your refusal will carry a tinge of hesitation or hostility.

There are bound to be some situations like these four examples when the other person may well feel rejected by your refusal, even though *you* may be clear that you are not rejecting them. Although there will be times when this can be used to manipulate you into changing your mind, this does bring up the issue of priorities. Only you can decide what is important enough for you to risk saying 'no' for – time on your own, privacy, spending your social time with people you want to be with – only you know how important each issue is on each separate occasion. When you have made that decision, you can act responsibly. You do not need to shut out the other person and pretend they do not matter. It is often very important to invite them to express what they feel as well. Once you feel assured that you have made the right decision for yourself, you can acknowledge that someone is angry or disappointed or upset without immediately trying to appease your own guilt. Nor do you have to make excuses but accept that this is your decision and stand by it. One final important point. When you do not remain true to your own needs and wishes, when you put aside a heartfelt 'no' for a half-hearted 'yes', do not kid yourself that it does not matter. The heartfelt 'no' will seek expression through some outlet. A refusal if not open and direct will always emerge somehow indirectly.

The indirect 'no'. Have you ever sulked or bitched your way through an evening when you did not really want to be there? Have you ever left a job to the last minute, or done it badly, or forgotten about it because you did not want to do it in the first place? Have you turned up late to a meeting because you did not want to attend or lost an address when you didn't want to go?

Sometimes we use our bodies to say 'no': headaches and backaches appear with miraculous timing when they can provide an unimpeachable excuse for not attending a function we should have said 'no' to in the first place.

And how does it feel to be on the receiving end of an indirect 'no'? How do you feel when someone cancels at the last minute with an excuse you know is a fake? How do you feel when someone has agreed to help and then does not turn up? Most of us have experienced let-down and disappointment and even fury with people who did not say a clear honest 'no' *at the time.*

There is security in knowing that you can trust someone to say what they mean; that they will say 'yes' when they mean 'yes' and 'no' when they mean 'no'. Instead of feeling guilty for accepting someone's help, you can allow yourself the pleasure of knowing they were free to choose.

The advantage of saying 'no' assertively is that you have more time to spend on things you want to say 'yes' to, instead of wasting time trying to extricate yourself from various unwanted commitments. And even if you feel guilty as you first try an assertive refusal, you will find that it gets easier with practice. You can survive the guilt and enjoy the reward of making a clean, honest decision.

Following on

Take situations from your own list or use the following suggestions:

a) A salesman at your door wants to sell you encyclopaedias.

b) You are in a shop and the saleswoman has been very helpful – she is urging you to take the dress you have tried on but you do not like it. Your goal is to refuse politely but firmly and leave the shop.

c) Your child asks for some more money to buy some sweets.

d) You are exhausted and have looked forward to a weekend of rest and solitude. On Thursday evening the telephone rings: an elderly relative wants to come and stay. Your task is to say no.

e) A friend asks to borrow a record of yours. You do not like lending out your records because they always seem to get damaged and so you want to refuse.

Checkpoints. Invite comments on your body language. Can you look the person in the eye as you say no? Do you smile inappropriately as you say no? Is your voice assertive or aggressive? Do you speak firmly or does your refusal contain a question? Can you say no without over-apologizing?

8

The Compassion Trap

It is easy to feel guilty about failure, faults and weakness. Guilty about letting others down, behaving uncaringly, being a disappointment, being selfish. Above all, guilty when you *don't care*.

The compassion trap is usually defined as a sense of obligation that, as a woman, you should put everyone else's needs before your own *all* of the time. You should always be available and accessible to others.

I see this as deeply rooted in a psycho-social legacy inherited from our mothers, grandmothers and no doubt many generations before that. The inherited image is of archetypal woman as a central, nurturing powerful force in the family. She is the focal point of the family. She is at home, bearing children: her task is to make sure that there is food on the table, that her husband's needs are anticipated and met; and it is her function to be a homemaker with whatever slender resources are available to keep the family together at all costs. She is the emotional centre, the heart of the family, while the men busy themselves with work and industry and moneymaking in other spheres. It is to her that the children turn first, with problems, physical and emotional bruises, tears to be kissed away by her. It is to her that the man turns for consolation and relief. She sees herself as a tower of strength, a refuge for those she loves.

Her life reflects the success and failure of her husband and her children. The best piece of meat goes to him, then her children – not because she feels inferior but because that's the way it is and always has been. They need the best. She can manage. Her whole life energy is expressed in this tenderness, this love and devotion which nourishes her family. In turn, her own sense of pride and satisfaction depends on the knowledge of giving this to them all, of feeding and watching them grow, taking their strength from her. This is fulfilment.

Some things have changed. Many women feel restless and are impatient. The family no longer represents total fulfilment for every woman. We want more but are not sure what it is. We begin to find new ways of self-expression, we move forward in search of understanding and meaning. But, uncertain and usually unsupported, we retreat in panic to the tower. We may talk of equality of status, work, pay; we talk of equal rights in life but there are very strong threads which bind us emotionally to that archetypal image.

These threads can bind us whether we're single or married, with or without children. However far removed is the reality of our own lives from the picture of the archetypal earthmother, we still run the risk of falling into similar traps, simply by being *women*.

Even without a real family, we can contrive to make ourselves indispensable to a 'family' of others in need: even without real children to care for, we can find others to love and look after with sacrifice and devotion. Even without a husband to defer to, we still allow our own needs and wants to go second. Intent on being selfless, we easily become over-stretched and exhausted by our responsibilities – at a cost to our own physical and mental well-being.

But, how, you may be asking, does this affect *me*? How can I tell when I am caught in the compassion trap?

As you read through the list below, see if you can recognize yourself or other women in these examples.

Situations with strangers. The patient who does not want to worry the over-worked nurses with a request for medication to relieve her own considerable pain; the customer who realizes that others have been waiting a long time so she does not take the time to get what she really wants; the passer-by who feels guilty if she passes by a blind man or begging child without giving some money which she can ill afford; the woman who reluctantly accepts a new hairstyle because she doesn't want to offend the enthusiastic new stylist.

Situations with friends. The woman who consistently makes excuses for a friend's hurtful behaviour rather than mentioning it directly; the woman who has sex with her boyfriend because he is turned on and she feels sorry for him; the woman who is afraid to refuse a friend who wants to come and stay at a thoroughly inconvenient time, because she knows her friend has been recently divorced and needs someone to talk to; the woman who feels guilty if she does not offer a lift to a friend because she is the only one with a car; the woman who has a talent for car maintenance or sewing and feels resentful but unable to refuse constant requests from friends to have 'a quick look' at their engines or replace a broken zip; Mrs X at Number 5 who does not like to refuse the invitation from Mrs Y at Number 7 to a Christmas drink every year because, even though it is a terrible bore, her neighbour might be offended . . . And then, of course, there is Mrs Y at Number 7 who does not like to stop inviting Mrs X at Number 5 because, even though it is a terrible bore, her neighbour might be offended!

Situations at home. The woman who has sacrificed her whole career to look after her invalid parents; the woman who will not share with her child her feelings of anxiety or frustration because she feels her daughter is too young to understand or cope; the wife who feels too guilty about leaving her housebound disabled husband to go out and enjoy herself for the day; the mother who refuses offers of help with a handicapped child because she feels she is the only one who must look after him; the daughter who does not like to tell her elderly father that he really should not drive any more as his sight is failing, because she knows he will feel upset about getting old and decrepit; the woman who feels guilty about enjoying her career so does not ask for the help she needs at home; the woman who does not ask her tenant to pay rent arrears because she feels sorry for her having a hard time with her boyfriend.

Situations at work. The woman who will not move to a more rewarding and stimulating job because she is convinced that this would leave her boss or colleagues 'in the lurch'; the doctor who will not accept that she needs holiday time like anyone else and allows herself to be available to patients 365 days a year; the sympathetic woman who sorts out others' problems during the lunch hour and after work because she has a reputation for being a good listener and cannot refuse; the older woman who will stay late at the office, correcting the work of junior colleagues: she does not like to tell them because they are young with busy social lives to lead; the librarian who does not like to tell the students not to smoke in the library: she sympathizes with their need to smoke when they are studying even though she knows it is her duty to make sure the rules are observed; the secretary who will not tell her boss he has made a mistake because it might deflate his ego.

You should by now have a few ideas! Let us have a look at how our four characters might deal with a situation of being caught in the compassion trap.

The Compassion Trap and a Passive, Aggressive, Indirect and Assertive Response

Dulcie's nineteen-year-old student nephew asks her to lend him some money to go abroad. It means giving him her savings for her own holiday, but she feels sorry for him and a little sensitive about being selfish – after all, she only has herself to think of as she does not have any children of her own, so she gives it to him. She swallows her disappointment and her resentment but holds close to her for a long time the hurt that he doesn't write to thank her. Even his parents do not show much appreciation of her gesture!

Agnes will often let her resentment build up to a tremendous outburst instead of appropriately saying 'no' beforehand. She eagerly takes up the cause of an 'unfortunate' friend who needs her help to make an entree into the world of her own business. She rushes around giving her advice, generously giving time and energy and suggestions, always being available when her friend rings up. Somehow the friend never really expresses appreciation, and Agnes begins to feel more and more used. Finally she erupts in fury, lambasts her friend and then drops her like a hot brick.

Ivy's way of dealing with the compassion trap is similar to Agnes's, but her strategies tend to be more hidden and indirect. When her next-door neighbour's husband leaves her, Ivy feels very sympathetic and listens to endless post mortems and all the ins and outs of their married life together. But after a few weeks she becomes frustrated that the neighbour will not do anything except moan. Ivy, unable to express her feelings directly, simply pretends not to be at home or, as soon as her friend appears, finds an excuse for going out.

Selma sits through her last committee meeting having decided after a lot of consideration to resign from her position as chairperson. She simply feels that an awful lot of her time has been given to chairing meetings, and she wants to conserve some of her energy and spend some time on things that are personally important to her. During the meeting, members plead with her not to go and ask if she can stay on for another few months: the committee's falling apart; they don't know how to cope without her. As Selma listens, she feels herself teetering on the edge of the trap. She finds herself in the midst of feelings that she ought to stay, as she is needed, and sympathy for her colleagues. Is she being selfish? Maybe she should just carry on for a few more months. But fortunately she keeps out of the trap and assertively maintains her decision. The others realize she is adamant and respect her decision – with regret. She leaves and is satisfied that she has done the right thing for herself.

Are you trying to be Superwoman?

Superwoman is selfless and has no needs of her own.

A fundamental premise which seems to pervade many of the compassion trap situations is that selflessness is always best. Although it is easy to admire someone's eager and selfless devotion to others, human martyrs often make others feel beholden to them and guilty in some way. If you have ever caught yourself sulking because someone wasn't sufficiently grateful to you for something you had done for them, then you can count yourself as playing the role of martyr. Can anyone ever be really appreciative enough?

It is unlikely that when we play the martyr, we do not expect *some* reward for all our devotion. Have you ever caught yourself secretly wounded or annoyed because someone did not notice the trouble you had taken or the effort you had made? However much we protest, it is difficult to claim to be totally altruistic – there is usually some reward in it for us.

And let's face it – it is uncomfortable being in the company of a martyr. You never know how or when they are going to want to be paid back.

The second apparent attribute of Superwoman is that she has no needs of her own. We will look at the dangers of thinking yourself inexhaustible in Chapter 13. If you find that getting stuck in the compassion trap means you are unable to say 'enough is enough', consider an assertive option:

Setting limits. This means calling a halt *before* you drop dead with exhaustion. Instead of waiting to the bitter end, you can look at ways in which you can ask for help, for support and for care from others. You can set limits on how you spend your time. You can give yourself the time to rest, to replenish your energy. You can allow yourself to be vulnerable like everyone else. Your needs are not necessarily more important than anyone else's needs – nor are they less important – just *equally* important. Letting go of the image of being a tower of strength gives everyone a chance to breathe a sigh of relief – you are seen to be human as well!

Setting limits also means looking to see whether you are taking your responsibilities too far. There is a fundamental difference here between taking care of someone's practical needs and someone's emotional needs. Of course there are times in everyone's life when they are practically dependent on another person's care. But if those limits are not recognized then the dependency slips into dangerous areas. Authentic care becomes displaced by subtle oppression. Oppression begins when you start assuming total responsibility for someone's emotional needs as well; when you deny them equal rights of interaction; when you take other people's decisions for them, and organize their lives on their behalf, because you assume they could not manage on their own.

There are two complementary roles. If someone is to play and remain the *inadequate*, then the other person can play and remain the *powerful*. Many women are reluctant to relinquish this power. This is understandable, since they do not feel powerful in any other area of their lives.

As women take more and more power for themselves assertively they will be more and more willing to relinquish this strong manipulative power and claim real equality.

I would like to finish this chapter by reassuring all those readers who indignantly affirm their role of Lady Bountiful. Avoidance of the compassion trap does not prevent you from showing compassion, and giving love and pleasure to other people. Compassion is undeniably a very beautiful quality.

But the quality suffers if there is no choice. Take an example: one of Celia's incessant complaints is having to take tea with her elderly Uncle Stan every Thursday. It cuts into her day, she complains, it prevents her from making other arrangements and she feels it is an inescapable burden. Once she has explored other options instead of moaning about it – refusing his invitation, reducing the visits to once a month instead of once a week, or asking a cousin to take over some of the visits – she finally decides that she is really very fond of her Uncle and that he isn't going to live long so she really wants to continue her visits. This is her choice. The arrangement continues to give him pleasure at her visit and attention, and to give her the pleasure of being able to do that for him.

If a woman feels compelled to put another's needs before her own, compassion becomes a sterile trap. If she is selective, and chooses awarely, the rewards and joys are rich and fertile.

9

Expressing Your Feelings

Most men and women feel very much at the mercy of their feelings. They approach their own and other people's feelings with the same mixture of awe and apprehension with which, if they were cast on to the ocean in a small sea-going vessel, they might view the rise and fall of the threatening waves around them. They have learned that there are currents to avoid; they can recognize imminent storm clouds. But, always prone to some unexpected turbulence and drama, they are tense and watchful. They know that ultimately they have no control. The best they can do is to guide their frail and inadequate craft over the water, often getting splashed, and occasionally capsizing, and always immensely thankful for a period of calm.

If you have ever felt at the mercy of your feelings or struggled to control them for fear they might overwhelm you, you will recognize the importance of being able to manage them effectively. Competence in managing feelings first requires some understanding of what feelings are all about. This chapter is especially relevant to assertiveness training. You need to know how to identify your feelings in order to know how to express them assertively.

What causes feelings? We generally accept that some kind of extreme emotion is to be expected when we experience a particular drama in our lives – such as the death of a loved one, falling in love, the shock of a bad car accident, the birth of a baby. But we tend to ignore the feelings triggered by minor events in our lives. The ordinary, everyday experience of interacting with other human beings – whether or not they are important to us – gives us plenty of scope to experience feelings.

Feelings are related to needs. Let us start with the need to give and receive love. If this need is fulfilled, we experience closeness, harmony, intimacy, belonging, togetherness, warmth and affection. If the need is not met or comes to an end for some reason, we experience sadness, pain, longing, emptiness, rejection, loneliness, we feel the grief of separation. A second need is to make choices, to be self-directing in our lives – positive feelings connected with this need are power, strength, enthusiasm, determination, energy, fulfilment, satisfaction, elation – or if the need is blocked, we experience frustration, impatience, helplessness, irritation, fury, outrage, anger. A third need to understand moves us to enquire and seek information and to communicate. Satisfying this need makes us feel safe, secure, it gives us a feeling of belonging. When we feel understood, we feel valued, acknowledged, certain and accepted for who we are. If we do not understand or are unable to communicate, we feel anxious, lost, confused, panicky, isolated, fearful and afraid.

The depth and quality of our feelings can vary widely. The ending of a wonderful holiday makes us feel sad, but the ending of a close relationship makes us grieve intensely. An affectionate letter from a friend makes us feel warm; a spontaneous hug from a child touches a deeper level of love. If we are in a hurry and the tin-opener will not work or the traffic lights are red, we feel impatient and frustrated. But if we are cheated out of monies due to us, or fall victim to bureaucratic stupidity or racial discrimination, our anger will strike a deeper chord. The satisfaction which follows the mastery of a new skill or the pride in accomplishing a very difficult task illustrate how we can feel when we are in command. The fear which is elicited by not knowing can range from anxiety about getting lost in unknown territory, to alarm if your child is very late home, or horror if you discover a mysterious lump in your breast. On the other hand, the security that comes from knowing exactly what you are doing, the delight in talking with someone who is on the same wavelength, the impact of an important insight, are all ways of experiencing the joys of understanding.

One single event can affect different needs at the same time. Take, for example, a young child whose mother dies. She will feel grief through the separation and loss of her mother; she will feel frightened because she cannot make sense of the meaning of death and does not know what will happen to her; she will probably feel angry with her mother for 'leaving' her in this way, and she will feel helpless in the new situation.

Exploring our feelings and experience can be a useful start to unravelling the complexity of what and why we feel the way we do.

Feelings are physical. Expressions such as 'I don't know what came over me', or 'I wasn't myself', or 'I was beside myself with rage' suggest that feelings are vague, ethereal presences which exist *outside* our bodies: that they descend and take us over; that they catch us unawares. In fact, what we experience as a feeling is a combination of sensations produced by physiological changes *inside* our bodies. Something happens to stimulate the brain to signal the release of chemical substances through particular organs. These chemicals produce a change in the body, preparing the body for appropriate action.

This is a very simplified and incomplete description of a highly complex chain of events. The important piece of information at this point is that a feeling is not something which can be dismissed as imagination – it is a real, physical, internal response. If you look at the diagram on page 63, you'll see that every feeling is represented by a physical sensation in our bodies. Although individual variations are inevitable, we can usually recognize the type of sensation which accompanies a particular category of emotion.

The bodily sensations associated with loving and being loved include the rush of love and affection, a bursting heart, an urge to sing, to dance, to bubble over – a feeling of head-to-toe vitality and energy, a lightness, a warm glow, a feeling of health, sexiness, radiance. And with the physical wrench of parting, we feel apathy, listlessness, light tears, or sobbing, emptiness – we want to curl up, we ache in our heart and our guts, we feel heavy.

If we are confused and fearful, we feel shaky, sweaty, we experience 'butterflies', goose-pimples, a tightness in our stomach and shoulders; a pounding heart, clammy hands, nausea, diarrhoea, trembling, shivering, numbness, we can feel paralysed, immobile or overcome with weariness.

People rarely have voluntary control over what they feel. Although they can control how they *act* on their feelings, they cannot be blamed or criticized for the feelings themselves.

Feelings come in for quite a battering; they are labelled childish, ridiculous, far-fetched, shameful, unfair or crazy. If unleashed they are alleged to cause unseemly or undignified behaviour; they are culturally approached with suspicion and distaste and, most reprehensible of all, feelings are thought to be *unreasonable*. So,

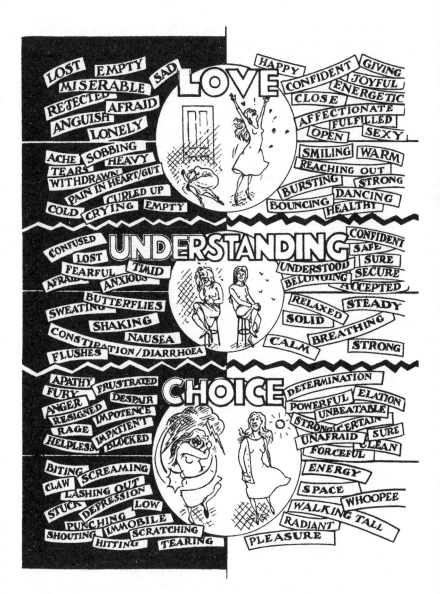

most of the time, most of us try to hide our feelings, even from ourselves.

Have you ever denied what you felt because, on the surface, it seemed illogical? Or reproached yourself because you felt guilty or ashamed or stupid for having certain feelings? Have you ever tried, for example, to dismiss the rejection you felt when you were criticized by someone on the grounds that they did not matter to you anyway? Or pretended you did not feel jealous when your partner was attracted to someone else because you wanted to appear liberated and 'together'? Have you tried to reason your way out of the feeling of frustration by counting your blessings instead? Or felt ashamed of wanting to hit out angrily at a helpless small child because you felt so frustrated? Have you ever denied feeling hurt because you thought you were just being too sensitive? Or felt too embarrassed to admit to feeling afraid or lonely and ask for comfort and support?

If your answer is 'yes' to any of the above questions you will be aware that not only is it futile to deny your feelings but also keeping them hidden makes them much harder to manage. They build up and after a while seem uncontrollable. Once you can accept that your feelings are real even if they do not make sense, when you can let yourself 'off the hook' for feeling something you would rather not admit to, then you can learn to identify what it is you feel, to trust your perception and go on to express your feelings assertively.

Three Levels of Expression

Expression of feelings can be handled at three different levels. First, all you need to do is simply notice and acknowledge to yourself what is going on. No one else need be made aware of it. A private acknowledgement can help you change your behaviour accordingly. You can leave the room, change the subject, breathe deeply, relax or whatever.

The second level is verbal expression. This can be just a simple statement: 'I feel hurt by that comment', 'That makes me very angry', 'I feel pressurized', 'I feel appreciated', 'I feel intimidated', 'I feel very warm towards you'.

The third level of expression involves the physical release of feelings – through tears or shouting or trembling.

It is important to know that feelings just do not go away. However much we wish them to disappear, however much we ignore, repress, deny, pretend or hide them away, feelings will find expression *somehow*. Taking a deep breath and counting to ten can help temporarily. There are many methods of stress-reduction currently available, which promote relaxation, meditation and exercise as ways of dealing with the anxieties and frustrations of our lives. But it is unlikely that we can eliminate *all* stressful feelings in these ways. I am convinced that unexpressed emotions will push for expression through another outlet. A pattern of physical and psychological symptoms will appear – constant low energy and fatigue, depression, withdrawal from contact with loved ones, headaches, vaginal infections, cystitis, backaches, skin irritations are examples of these symptoms.

What holds us back from this third level of expression? A major inhibition stems from a fear that for an adult to express feelings openly is childish and shameful. And this fear is endorsed by our experience with other adults – instead of compassion and acceptance, tears in an adult are met with alarm and embarrassment; instead of respect and understanding, they elicit pity and suspicion. As very young children, we were able to express our feelings quite openly and spontaneously without shame. Although we have had to learn to control our feelings as part of growing up, most of us have learned to over-control them to such an extent that we are now no longer aware of even having any feelings, let alone being able to identify and express them.

Relearning how to express our feelings is an important step. It is also helpful to learn how to unlock and release the pent-up feelings from the past. Many of us store a lot of unexpressed emotions, some stimulated by recent events and others caused by events experienced long ago in childhood. These feelings can undermine our relationships with others without our realizing it. Releasing past, unexpressed feelings can help us arrive at a better understanding of ourselves and can open the door to self-expression and fulfilment.

The exploration of this relationship between past experiences and present behaviour is beyond the scope of an assertiveness training class. But it is still relevant for us to realize how our feelings affect our behaviour and that if we do not acknowledge them to ourselves or express them verbally to another person, they will distort our communication and behaviour.

This will occur frequently when dealing with anxiety. When learning to say 'no' or to make a difficult request, we understandably feel awkward, embarrassed or nervous. Those feelings can paralyse us with anxiety and most of us try to hide this. The result is reduced effectiveness in the interaction. Anxiety unexpressed will emerge in a variety of ways – a peremptory manner, stilted voice, condescending tone, jerky movements are examples.

Self-disclosure. The best way to handle this is to disclose what you are feeling with a verbal statement. For instance: 'I feel nervous coming to talk to you about money but I want to ask for a raise', 'I find it difficult to ask, but would you help me with this problem', 'I feel guilty at having to say no, but I must refuse'.

The *immediate* effect of this is to reduce your anxiety. It allows you to relax and take command of yourself. When we feel confident and secure, the overall physical sensation is relaxation. Everything starts flowing in the body again – we feel looser and stronger. As soon as you are relaxed, you will automatically deepen your breathing: this affects your voice which, with your gestures, can now convey a *totally* assertive message. The importance of this particular skill cannot be over-emphasized.

Karen wanted to practise asking two friends not to smoke in her sitting room. Whenever they asked if she minded, she never knew how to handle it. When she role-played the first time, she managed to say 'no' to her friends, but it sounded awkward and uncomfortable. The second time, she started off by saying, 'You know I feel really awkward saying this but I would prefer you not to smoke in here. I just don't like it.' As soon as she disclosed what she was feeling, she was more comfortable in handling the situation and the tension and stiffness disappeared.

You can apply this to any situation – you only have to recognize what you are feeling and then make a similar simple statement.

When we are angry, the information we need comes from our bodies. We feel hot, we go red in the face, we want to stamp or jump up and down. Or we may experience frustration when feeling helpless – in which case we will experience stodginess, the sensation of being hemmed in and stifled, we feel restricted, crushed, inert, blank. Feeling sad, disappointed, rejected has a different effect. Learn to identify what happens in your own body. Once you detect the physical sensation, you can recognize what you are feeling, and then respond appropriately. This may mean telling someone what you feel, taking a deep breath to calm yourself, having a good yell to relieve your frustration or sitting tight until you are in a safer place before letting go. Obviously you cannot just let go when you feel like it, but with the information about what is happening inside you, you can allow yourself to decide what to do in a particular situation, whereas simply denying your feelings makes life much more difficult.

It is easy to overestimate our ability to fool other people about what we are feeling inside. So although we think that with sufficient facial and vocal control, we can hide what is going on, little tell-tale signs on the outside will give us away: the inappropriate smile which masks unexpressed anger or grief or anxiety: tiny eye movements, gestures, the set of the jaw and especially the tone of voice. All these will betray your true feelings even if you are not consciously aware of them yourself.

Often in a role-playing situation, a woman will learn from other people's observations that her body is giving off all sorts of little signals about her feelings which she knows to be true although she finds it hard to admit them even to herself! Remember, you are not to blame for your feelings. What you feel is important. It may be silly, groundless, irrational. But if you feel it, it is real.

This ability to identify the feeling leads us to another problem. Many women experience a time lapse between the *experience* of an emotional response and the actual acknowledgement. We may experience a flash of feeling *at the time* although it may take hours, days or even months for the full burst of recognition to register. So we often have to be content with sighing 'If only I'd expressed what I felt', or 'If only I'd followed my impulse', 'If only I'd replied as I really wanted to'. We tend to agonize and spend a lot of time re-running the scene in our heads, enacting the part to perfection – with the other party suitably impressed, intimidated or penitent! With practice we can narrow the gap more and more until we are able to recognize our feelings immediately. In this way, we can develop a more spontaneous approach – whatever the feeling – whether resentment or affection, confusion or joy, we can just express it – and maybe act on it if we choose.

The value of feelings. As we learn to identify our feelings, we learn how valuable they are. Feelings can act as a vehicle of understanding the truth of what is really happening in a situation even though our heads may be telling us something different. It is very easy to dismiss what we feel because we do not have real evidence.

You may have experienced meeting someone for the first time and sensing with an absolute certainty that this person could be trusted. You may have felt suspicious or uncomfortable with someone's request even though you couldn't put your finger on exactly what was wrong. You may have made a decision in your life because you knew it was right for you even though you could not offer a satisfactory verbal explanation to anyone else – maybe not even to yourself.

In none of these situations do you have any real evidence of the sort that would stand up in court. You simply know what you feel to be true. You just feel it. Feelings of this kind are called intuitive. Information obtained through intuition can complement what we can learn through our powers of reasoning and logic.

One of the difficulties in establishing the value of emotional intelligence is that both men and women have been steeped in the current cultural myth that what we know and understand through our emotions is of less significance than what we know through our physical senses. Because we cannot see, touch or measure feelings as easily as we can see and touch physical objects, we find our language inadequate to describe them. We cannot share our experience of emotion and intuition in the same way as we can identify with someone's physical experience of a cold shower or carrying a heavy weight. Scientific values have become over-important at the expense of intuition which is dismissed as trivial, frivolous or a quirk of the imagination because we have no *proof* – or at least not the sort of proof that others may need to understand that what we are talking about is *real*.

Furthermore, since the area of emotion and intuition has been traditionally the domain of the female, it has suffered, like the beauty and power of childbirth, from a process of social devaluation. The importance of education and training in emotional competence has been relegated to the bottom rung of the ladder of worthwhile and desirable human accomplishments. Intellectual skills have taken precedence over emotional skills: management of words and ideas, figures and objects earns acclaim – the skill of handling the expression of feelings competently within human relationships has become irrelevant.

Since feelings are powerful, people are frightened of them. And like anything else which defies ultimate control, we seek to restrain, deny and diminish their power. But when we cut ourselves off from what we feel, we also cut ourselves off from our emotional intelligence, and thus from an essential source of personal insight and guidance.

With the information in this chapter and with practice in expression, we can learn to trust our body cues and feelings, and to see and enjoy them as a valuable reliable source of information and learning. Instead of insisting that the head rule the heart, I believe that we should foster a collaboration between the two. Learning to acknowledge and express your feelings assertively is a vital part of this process.

.

10
The Two Faces of Anger

Of all our complex and powerful emotions, anger remains the most misunderstood. Whereas love is regarded as beautiful and enhancing, anger is considered ugly and degrading. We associate anger with the baser side of human nature, which is dark, sinister and threatening: a side we would rather not see or talk about. We bottle it up, turn a blind eye, sit on it or swallow it. We control angry feelings in whatever way we can and we encourage others to do the same. And it is because we neither acknowledge nor understand our anger that it remains for many people the most difficult of all the emotions to manage.

In the last chapter we saw that the range of feelings connected with frustration and anger were clustered around the need for self-expression and self-direction. In order to understand this in more depth, we need to look at two aspects of anger: a deep layer which contains a powerful source of energy and a top layer of past and present hurts and frustrations. Look at the diagram of the maze on page 71. Try to imagine yourself on the inside looking for a way through. The very fact that you want to find a way through shows that the first and deepest layer is operating inside you. Without it, you would just give up and lie down and die. But with it, you feel a wish to survive, to move forward, to develop, to change, to overcome difficulties, to discover, to get through. This movement is fuelled by a very deep and fundamental energy which keeps you going.

You may not be aware of it as a force inside you but you will

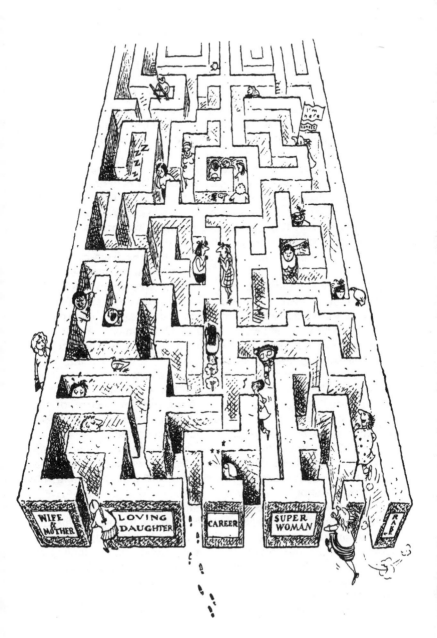

probably feel its effects. It provides the impetus to learn new skills – to master a complicated recipe, pass a driving test, to learn to communicate in another language; it pushes you to express yourself in writing or singing or painting; it can push you on in a career or to some goal that you see as fulfilling; because of it you can survive crises and disasters and illness; you make choices to read this book, leave a relationship, to take care of your body, start a business, to colour your hair, write a poem, attend a class, to say 'no' or 'yes' for yourself. This anger, which I call *root anger,* has, at its source, the basic *you,* the person under all the roles and responsibilities you assume in your life.

Imagine the figure in the diagram starting off through the maze. The signposts give an idea of the confusion of directions and conflict of goals that face many women today. Most of us use the experience and example of our mothers or other women as a starting point for our own journey. We may choose to follow suit or take a totally contradictory direction, depending on how we felt about what we saw and experienced. But as you can see from the diagram, many of the choices can be self-limiting. The woman in the maze may feel that marriage and motherhood is the right direction for her to take and then find herself, a few years later, unable to move any further. Or she may opt for a career or intellectual status and still find herself hemmed in and in some way frustrated. Or she may choose to go in more than one direction, or follow the path of loving daughterhood or the selfless spouse; or she may take the routes which promise approval like compassion or stoicism or superwoman or cover girl and *still* find herself, unfulfilled, at another dead end.

An added difficulty is that without the perspective of this diagram, all she can see when inside is the high walls. She often feels blocked, stuck and alone. If she bumps into another woman en route, as likely as not they will smile in sad recognition and shuffle on without a word or if they do converse, they will each pretend that they know *exactly* where they are going and part, humming with busy contentment.

It is within these walls, we encounter the source of the second kind of anger. Our actual experience of angry feelings of this kind will fall broadly into two types: one stems from the desire to tear down the walls and the other describes the despair at feeling the walls are immovable. We feel powerful or powerless. We tend to swing from one to the other and we may experience wanting to hit out at those walls, whatever they represent in our lives. We may see them as society, our parents, our children, all men, our employers, whoever we see as responsible for blocking our movement, impeding our progress, stopping us from doing what we want, holding us back, restricting our freedom. We want to break them down and destroy them, hurt them as much as we have been hurt, stamp on them, break them, kill them.

And if we succeed (which is unlikely) then we find only more walls or we feel very remorseful for the damage we have done. Or we just get tired of banging away at those walls, and feel very alone. We feel helpless, that it is useless to try; we lose heart, we stop fighting, we become immobile and apathetic and sink back in despair and resignation.

Most of us alternate between these two extremes – aggressive or passive. Either way we remain ineffectual. A major problem is that some of the aggression is what I have just described as root anger. Some of the stress we feel *enables* us to move forward – it motivates us to change our lives and we do not want to lose that. But it becomes so bound up with wanting to hit out and blame and take revenge that, in fear of our violence, we repress everything. The combination of the general taboo on the expression of anger in our culture plus a further discouragement, as women, from showing that side of ourselves, has meant that we have lost contact with not only our destructive anger but also a fundamental source of energy and purpose. And it is hardly surprising we have lost touch with a lot that is powerful in us, especially when we are more often encouraged to be loving, compassionate and caring than direct, vigorous, determined, outspoken, fearless and creative. Most women have been discouraged from an early age from expressing anger directly. Here are some examples of such discouraging messages.

Count to twenty before you say anything.
It's unladylike to raise your voice.
You can only win if you don't lose control.
You're not a pretty sight when you're angry.
Go upstairs and stay there until you take that scowl off your face.
You sound like a fishwife.
You're being hysterical.

Do you worry that it is arrogant, undignified or unfeminine to express anger? Do you fear losing control and unleashing a volcanic stream of molten lava which will destroy everything in its path? Do you fear provoking a violent response in the other person? Have you ever felt your robes of compassion wearing thin or becoming too tight or scratchy but have suffered discomfort because you did not want to appear harsh, uncaring, abrasive, domineering, threatening, aggressive or unwomanly?

If so, then you may be interested to learn that assertive expression of anger is possible. You can learn to express your anger cleanly and directly, without destroying or punishing yourself or anyone else in the process. And in doing so, you can begin to recover a powerful source of vitality, a sense of your own power and energy and identity.

The experience of frustration and anger is unavoidable in our lives. Simply wishing it away or turning a blind eye will not induce it to disappear. And even if you try hard to 'rise above it', you will only be able to rise so far before you come clattering down on some unsuspecting head. Facing your anger, taking charge of it, learning to express it cleanly without smearing it over everyone else's face is certainly a challenge. It is very difficult and takes courage and encouragement to take that first step.

The Expression of Anger

Let us look at how Agnes, Dulcie and Ivy handle their anger and frustration. How does it make itself felt in their lives?

Agnes. Agnes uses aggressive tactics to express her rage. The effect at the receiving end is similar to the sensation of being punched hard with a series of blows from a heavyweight boxer. You know exactly where it is coming from, you reel under the force of it; you may try and retaliate and protest or you may shield yourself from further damage. Agnes is quick to flare up – her resentment simmers just below the surface. So the slightest provocation can trigger the actual eruption although the hurt and frustration has been accumulating for quite a while. When someone moves out of line, says the wrong thing, makes a silly mistake or has a particular look in the eye, she over-reacts and attacks before she can be hurt any more. She often goes over the top and then feels remorseful afterwards when she surveys the damage. She feels helpless, angry, hurt and guilty. Furthermore she knows that the other person did not really hear what she was saying so she continues to nurse her grievance. This confusion can tip her into a Dulcie-like mood of despair and futility.

Dulcie. Dulcie wonders what the point is anyway. She has lost sight of her frustration. She does not have the energy to make much of a fuss any more. She still complains and moans about how she is treated unfairly but never to the person concerned. Dulcie's anger lies deeply buried like the winter earth under successive layers of snow. Occasionally she may lash out like Agnes, but will then feel guilty and reinforced in her conviction that there is no point in trying. Her unexpressed anger becomes a burden to herself and a burden to others. She drags the ball and chain with her, clinging on to those around her, slowing down their progress in turn. Her anger is conveyed through her silence and she often closes off from physical affection or sexual contact.

Ivy. The more her anger grows, the more Ivy tightens the reins of control on herself and others. Her unexpressed anger takes the shape of invisible poison darts – quick, apparently coming from nowhere, sudden, difficult to pinpoint and very painful on impact. They may appear as put-downs, be transmitted as 'a look that could kill', or feel more like a slap in the face – like forgetting something important to you, not turning up to an agreed meeting, betraying a confidence, making a fool of you in front of others, letting you know how inadequate or disappointing you are.

When we express anger we often swing from Agnes to Dulcie moods and commonly employ a variety of routines and strategies through which we express our anger and frustration indirectly. The following four imaginary characters given an idea of the sort of behaviour both women and men resort to when, for whatever reason, they feel unable to express these feelings directly.

The Disruptor. The disruptor is out to make mischief. Wherever a few are gathered, she can get to work. She will make an apparently innocent remark, ask a naive question or 'accidentally' let slip a remark or snippet of information and, very subtly, the seeds of doubt and anxiety are sown among her audience. Conflict is in the air. Hackles are raised; quarrels break out; disruption ensues. The result can be described as an interpersonal stink bomb. The disruptor plants it unnoticed and then withdraws as the invisible stench gathers strength. Although she may leave the situation behind, the odour lingers long after her departure.

The Spoiler. Somehow the spoiler always manages to choose the wrong moment to ask for something. You are settling down to watch a favourite television programme; you have just collapsed into an armchair in anticipation of a little relaxation; you are hopping with impatience to take off on a long-awaited holiday or outing . . . and along comes the spoiler. She will suddenly announce the arrival of your least favourite guests; or demand your attention for a pressing problem or help with a task that requires your immediate co-operation. Whenever you plan something important, she will sabotage it in some subtle way – a forgotten appointment, a late arrival, an incapacitating headache, a double booking. You start to share enthusiasm or talk interestedly with a friend – she will butt in with irrelevant comments. Her own frustrations and tension prevent her from being able to listen and without realizing what she is doing, she will find ways of spoiling things for others.

The Deflater. Whenever you are feeling on top of the world, you can be sure the deflater will bring you down. Your bubble will burst on the sharp edge of her tongue. You may be feeling proud of an achievement and really pleased with yourself: you will be met with a remark such as 'Well, I don't know what you're making such a fuss about. It wasn't *that* difficult.' You delightedly show her a new purchase when she says, 'How on earth could you afford it? I thought you said you were broke!' If you have clinched a deal or had a bit of luck, she will try and make you feel guilty with a well-aimed remark such as 'Some people are always lucky' or 'Well, it's all right for some'. You show her a new dress and she comments 'I see everyone's wearing that style these days'. Again her feelings of unfairness and resentment are expressed indirectly.

The Stoker. The stoker finds a channel for her frustration by driving everyone else up the wall. She will complain endlessly about her aches and pains or the wretchedness of her existence, listen with apparent interest to your suggestions but persistently refuse all offers of help; somehow she will get you going, she will remind you of past grievances and irritations, fuel your dislike of someone just to see you erupt in fury. She will play helpless martyr until you are beside yourself with rage and impotence. Whether the final eruption is towards her or towards another convenient target does not always matter. The important goal of this strategy is the experience of eruption by proxy. Someone else will get angry for her as long as she keeps stoking – many Agnes types settle in relationships with Dulcie types for this very reason.

We can recognize these characters and can identify with them. We have used them and been abused by them. Acknowledging them in our own behaviour makes it easier to understand what is happening when we find ourselves at the receiving end of similar indirect expressions of aggressive feelings.

Your Own Experience of Dealing with Anger

Who or what makes you angry? Injustice? Stupidity? Incompetence? Insensitivity? Lies? Bureaucracy? Snobbery? Untidiness? Prejudice? Waste? Cruelty? Hypocrisy? Being taken for granted? Being ignored? Being excluded? Not being listened to? Do you feel most strongly affected by people close to you? Those in your immediate family? Friends? Parents? Relatives? People far removed from you? People in authority? Particular professionals?

What are the signs that your body gives you when you are angry? Do you feel hot? Your heart pounds? Sweating? Tension in your jaw or shoulders? Do you feel like grabbing something or hitting out? Do you feel powerful? Frightened? Do you feel like stamping on something (or someone)? Are your fists clenched? Do you feel physically like breaking out? Needing air or space? Do you feel a rush of adrenalin?

When and with whom do you feel safe enough to express angry feelings? On your own, miles away from anywhere? With your family? A close friend? A lover or spouse? Men? Women? Your cat? With no one? With a large amount of alcohol inside you? In a letter? Never?

How do you express your feelings? This brings us to two separate needs – the need to release the energy physically and reduce the stress level in your body, and second, the need to confront the source of your anger.

This second need has two aspects: first, there is sometimes a need to confront someone immediately. This requires practice and conviction which relies on effective use of body language. Secondly, there is a need to confront the cause of our anger and frustration from a long-term perspective. We have to look at a situation or a relationship and take active steps towards eliminating or reducing the source of stress in that situation. This requires thought, care and skill and is not to be confused with dealing with your feelings in the heat of the moment. Confrontation skills are the subject of Chapter 12. The rest of this chapter looks at management of *immediate* feelings of anger – your own and others'.

Physical release. If you remember that expressing your frustration will also free the root anger in you, you will realize how important it is to give yourself permission for this kind of release. Obviously it may not be possible at the time. You may choose not to erupt in an important meeting or yell at the boss or hit out at your children or have a tantrum in the middle of the supermarket. The important thing to remember is that your body has a need and that even if you choose, at the time, what you consider to be a more appropriate and moderate form of expression, like breathing deeply, going for a short walk, focusing outside your distress, or counting to ten, it is important to make a mental note to give yourself some uninhibited 'release time' as soon as possible.

The following ways of 'letting go' are among those recommended by class participants: driving with the windows closed and yelling or screaming at the top of your voice; scrubbing the floor; kneading bread; slamming doors; going for a run; punching cushions; stamping or jumping up and down; strangling a towel; biting hard into a towel or screaming your head off; hitting the wall with an old tennis racket; driving fast (but take care!). You may have your own personal way of letting off steam – choose whatever works best for you.

The more often you allow yourself this space when you need it, the less you accumulate tensions and rage; the more accustomed you become to dealing with events as they happen, the lower you will keep the internal pressure. The other advantage is that it becomes easier to admit to being angry, at the time, assertively and clearly without precipitating an avalanche of stored-up tension.

How to communicate that you are angry. You can begin with a simple verbal statement such as 'I'm angry'. If you say this assertively, this may be sufficient to get your message across. If not, you can go further. You may need to add more force to your statement, but first you will have to be convinced yourself that you have had enough, that your limits have been reached, that you don't like what is happening, that you are angry. Once you are convinced, you can *hit the right note*.

Angry women often grit their teeth, swallow back and cry instead of getting angry. To make matters worse, we usually smile – a smile which stems from nervousness and a desire to placate. This confuses everyone because of the double message. If you want to be angry with conviction, you must first be aware of your smile. Remember it is only when your voice and body match the content of your speech that you make a clear, unequivocal impact. You may need to practise raising your voice level. Often we have become so rusty at using our voices that raising the volume seems physically impossible at first. But we need to push through the controlled and reasonable tones. Strength and conviction do *not* include sarcasm – this is where you need to be careful. A slight inflection of contempt or a sneer will undermine the assertive nature of your expression.

Once it tips over into hostility, the expression becomes aggressive rather than assertive. Hitting the right note has a lot to do with relaxation. When we are faced with a confrontation we are often paralysed by anxiety. Anxiety restricts our breathing: the throat tightens and our attempts to shout end only in producing a high-pitched squeak! Practise increasing the volume of your voice and learn that you can still have control of it. If you deepen your breathing, you will deepen the sound and the tone of your voice will be more effective.

Rising to the occasion. Sometimes, a situation demands that you accelerate to keep pace with the other person. In Pamela Butler's book, *Self Assertion for Women* she talks about 'muscle' which I have called *Gears*. This describes the process of escalation – you start off in a low gear, but may need to go up to a high gear if the situation requires it. Imagine a situation where you are confronted with something that starts off as a minor irritation but which increases until it becomes a full-blown major source of annoyance.

Say, for example, that you are in a cinema and a child is annoying you by kicking the back of your seat. You may turn round and say 'Would you please stop kicking my seat. It is disturbing me and I want to enjoy the film.' (*First gear.*) After all, the child may be doing so absent-mindedly, in which case turning round and bellowing might be excessive. Let's say though that the child hears you, but after a lapse of thirty seconds the same pattern of intermittent kicking begins again. This time you turn round and say, with your voice just a little louder and firmer, 'Would you *please* stop kicking my seat? I don't like being disturbed as I want to watch this film.' (*Second gear.*) After a further minute, the kicking resumes. By now you know that you have given the child the benefit of the doubt and that the irritation is deliberate. So you turn round and say in a very loud voice, 'Stop kicking my seat or I'll call the manager.' (*Third gear.*) There may be a petulant response or muttered curse but either way the kicking may stop at this point and your wish is met, which is to watch the film. If it does not stop at this point then you have to resort to *fourth gear* and actually call the manager and take the situation from there.

Disarming anger in others. Many women who come to the classes express a fear of dealing with anger in someone else.

If you want to interrupt a torrent of angry words or behaviour, first of all get the person's attention. Do this by repeating one word or a short phrase, like 'Listen to me', 'Stop that' or repeat the person's name. Repeat what you say over and over again, pitching your voice so that you will be heard.

The next move is to make eye contact. The sound of your voice and the repetition will probably make them look at you, maybe just for an instant, but once they look, hold their attention. Follow through *immediately* with a short phrase, whatever you want to communicate: for example 'I know you're angry. We'll talk later when you have calmed down', 'I know you're angry but I'm frightened when you're like this'.

If you follow through immediately, the other person will hear you and then you have a chance to communicate.

When you practise this in role-play (and it is essential to practise this beforehand) you may find that, being unfamiliar with the power of your own voice, you are quite startled when the other person stops. At this point, you may back away, dumbstruck. Practice will help you to follow through at that vital moment. One final point: if you try and it does not work and the person continues regardless, then remember you always have an option to leave.

We looked at how anxiety can keep us rooted to the spot when saying 'no' to someone. Similarly, we feel compelled to hear the person out, to suffer the abuse to the bitter end, when it may be more assertive simply to go away.

Disarming someone else who is angry needs care and skill but most important is the way you handle your own angry feelings. You will automatically feel more comfortable and confident in handling angry scenes with others when you are less afraid of being able to give full vent to the expression of anger yourself.

11

How to Handle Criticism

Few of us welcome criticism with open arms. If caught unawares by a critical comment we feel stung; if we know it is coming in advance, we feel anxious and defensive. Our current response to criticism is based on the experience of being criticized in the past – maybe a week ago, a year ago, even thirty years ago.

Childhood experience of criticism can be an important insight into the assertive management of criticism; both how to respond to someone's criticism of you and how to give critical feedback to someone else. It is a very sensitive area and one which class participants often find difficult to handle. It means looking at the vulnerable places within each of us which we may prefer to avoid. But avoiding criticism is what most of us do already. We stop ourselves from saying what we want to say, doing what we want to do, living how we want to live, being who we want to be . . . simply to avoid criticism and disapproval.

Why does criticism hit so hard? Why does the very word 'criticism' have such a nasty ring to it? Pause for a while and review your past experiences of criticism, particularly those of your childhood, and see if you can identify with any of the following: being made to look foolish when making a mistake; the ominous comment on a school report about being lazy or a bad influence; being scolded for getting dirty or shouting back; being punished for being jealous and spiteful or ridiculed for getting low marks; belittled for being childish because you were afraid of the dark and did not want to be left alone.

The first, almost universal, element in our experience of criticism is labels. Few parents heed the principle that they should criticize the behaviour, not the child. So what most of us have experienced as criticism when we were children was labelling: 'you're stupid', 'you're clumsy', 'you're a nuisance', 'you're a show-off', 'you're deceitful', 'you'll never be as good as your sister', 'you're selfish', 'you're a real burden to your mother'. It was not simply that you had done something silly or said something unkind – it actually meant that you were fundamentally stupid and bad!

The second element in the criticism we experienced as children, and in the criticism we continue to experience today, is *rejection*. When someone criticizes us, we do not experience this as a loving approach, designed to benefit us, but as disapproval, punishment, a withdrawal of affection and love – sometimes total annihilation. And, almost always, we are *right* in experiencing criticism as negative and unloving because that is exactly what it is. From our childhood experiences stems our anticipation of criticism as rejection. This is reinforced by more recent experiences of the same kind.

Both giving and receiving criticism tends to be handled very badly. To get a better idea of how your childhood experiences affect your adult reaction to criticism, try to imagine yourself experiencing criticism now. See if you can identify with the six-year-old thoughts and feelings of the following three little girls.

'You wait!' . . . an Agnes in the making: 'How dare you call me stupid. I'm not stupid. You're stupid. What's wrong with it anyway? Ouch! I always get hit. That hurts. You just wait until I get bigger. Then I'll bash you. I'll hurt you more. I'll make you sorry. You'll see. Just because you're a grown-up . . . you just wait!'

'It's not fair' . . . an Ivy in the making: 'It wasn't my fault. He started it anyway. You're just picking on me. It's always *me*. You never see the good things. What do you mean, take that look off my face? I just hate you. Still, I'd better look as if I'm sorry. But I'm not really. It's just not fair . . .'

'I just can't help it' . . . a Dulcie in the making: 'I can't help making mistakes. I can't help being clumsy . . . how was I to know it was so important? I can never seem to do the right thing. You're always getting at me. If I weren't here, *then* you'd be happy. You just don't love me any more. Why do I have to keep getting everything wrong? It's not really my fault. I just can't help it.'

You may recognize yourself in all three of them. Some of the same thoughts and feelings of the young Agnes, Ivy and Dulcie creep into our approaches as adults. We can easily end up struggling to manage criticism as an intelligent adult, yet inside be experiencing the feelings and attitudes more appropriate to the six-year-old child.

The adult Agnes will claim to be impervious to criticism. She regards criticism as nothing but an attack and since she spent so much time in the powerless position, now has to make sure that she wins. So she immediately retaliates with 'How dare you!' or 'It's your fault'. She will not hear of being at fault herself. All the helplessness wells up in her and she has to prove herself the winner every time.

The adult Ivy will also refuse to let in the truth of the criticism because her sense of unfairness is stirred up. Although she may adopt a suitably penitent expression and silently 'suffer' accusation, she will get her own back with a subtle character attack later on when her critic is not looking.

And Dulcie? She does not receive criticism either. She immediately crumples, too readily she agrees that yes, she is a nasty person, she is no good, she really is a failure. Anything valid that her critic is saying is likely to sink without trace in the general swamp of her self-pity and self-reproach.

We have learnt to mistrust people who criticize us. We anticipate an attack: we expect to have to defend ourselves, so the minute we suspect the criticism is coming, psychologically we arch our backs. We are also very suspicious about the slightest possibility of oneupmanship or that the other person is trying prove themselves superior to us in some way. By acknowledging the truth of what they are saying it feels as if we have 'lost' and they have 'won'. This is why criticism is such a sensitive area – a veritable minefield. These difficulties are perpetuated by the way most adults handle giving criticism to each other. Most people – whether our friends, lovers, spouses, employers – will still use labels and often consider themselves as self-appointed judges of our behaviour. But even though you cannot expect others to be skilled in handling criticism, you can still learn to handle criticism assertively yourself.

An Assertive Approach to Criticism

The first step is to distinguish between criticism which is valid, criticism which is invalid, and criticism which is nothing but a thinly veiled put-down.

There's a good chance that the ways we coped with criticism as children . . .

. . . will be carried over into our adult lives

Valid criticism is criticism which you know to be legitimate. You *did* make a mess of that job; you *have* arrived late too often; you *did* forget an important letter; you *do* change your mind a lot; you *are* putting on weight; you *are* fussy . . . whatever it is, you know that it is true and does apply to you.

Handling these criticisms requires the skill of *negative assertion*. Negative assertion helps you to handle either hostile i.e. badly managed criticism, or constructive criticism i.e. criticism from a person who has your own interests at heart and is not simply out to get you. Negative assertion is learning how to agree with the criticism, if it applies to you, and to recognize it to be legitimate. For example, 'Yes, I am untidy'; 'Yes, I agree, I did make a mess of that last piece of work'. You do not have to melt into a pool of self-deprecation and abject apology. Nor do you turn round and say 'how dare you'. You can simply acknowledge the truth in what your critic is saying. Then you can feel less defensive and more accepting of yourself. I sometimes encourage class members to add a phrase with which they feel comfortable. For example, if someone criticizes you for being inconsistent, and secretly you rather enjoy this particular quirk in your personality, there is no point in saying 'Yes, you're right, I'm terribly sorry' when it would be more honest to say 'Yes, I am inconsistent and I rather like that in me, I think it's very creative'. If on the other hand someone criticizes you about something you are aware of trying to improve, you can always add that too. For example, you might say 'Yes, I am too aggressive, you're right. I sometimes find it difficult to be assertive. But I'm practising and getting better!'

Invalid criticism. This category of criticism includes those comments or accusations which you know to be absolutely untrue. But instead of coming straight out and saying so, you may find that your first reaction is to consider it legitimate simply because someone has stated that it is so! If someone calls you 'mean', for example, when you know that meanness is not one of your 'vices', instead of refuting the comment in a convincing manner, you may hesitate. Then you will remember the two occasions when you *were* mean and accept the criticism as justified, even though you feel it is unfair. If it does not belong to you, you do not have to work hard to try and make it fit! Try saying something like 'That's completely untrue! On the contrary . . .' 'I don't accept that at all'. Say it with conviction, not apology. Make sure your total body language expresses certainty rather than doubt.

Put-downs. 'The trouble with you is you've got no sense of humour!' Put-downs are extraordinarily slippery. The time lapse we have talked about between reaction and response is very pertinent to the experience of being put-down. Perhaps you do not register at the time, but then wake up in the middle of the night thinking 'What the hell did she mean?' Of if you *do* register that you are angry or hurt by a comment, and venture to say so, you may be met with retorts of 'You're imagining it – it was just a joke', or 'Why do you have to take everything so seriously/personally?'

This is effectively a double put-down. It hooks into a secret fear that you really are over-sensitive, that your feelings are bizarre and that you do not have the intelligence to hear what you hear or see what you see. Often in a class, participants are invited to contribute to a put-down parade. Because we experience so many put-downs in common, this has the effect of reassuring people that they are *not* imagining things and they can draw reassurance and support from others' experience, that they are not simply over-imaginative or paranoid.

Some people suggest that the best way to deal with put-downs is by some clever cutting remark that will instantly wither the speaker. I am not convinced that this is in fact the best way. Although there are some very brilliant and amusing examples often quoted and re-quoted in company, not all of us have that talent. I also believe that teaching women how to cap one put-down by another is more competitive than assertive. So I suggest the following:

If you think you are just being baited then hold your ground if you can and express your reaction assertively, using the gears if you need to. If you do not manage it, then do not reproach yourself too much. Once you are certain of how you feel, you can take the time to confront the person later and tell them assertively how you felt.

Whether criticism is valid or invalid or just a put-down, you will probably recognize that some areas are much more difficult to handle than others. And there are some which we do not want to look at at all. These are what I call *crumple-buttons*. This term describes those chinks in your defensive armour, where you are most vulnerable. We all have them. Words or phrases which are so highly sensitive that the mere mention has the effect of making you crumple instantly inside – you may feel utterly defeated, or hurt, or you fly off the handle; it may be a reference to your appearance and general manner: your colour, weight, dress sense, breast size, accent. It may be a reference to your background: class, race, education, accent, experience, qualifications. It may be a comment on a particular area of competence: as a mother, a lover, as a cook, intellectual, driver. It may be a specific word: such as selfish, over-bearing, hard, stupid, aggressive, tight.

Whatever the word or phrase, you will recognize its impact. It does not matter if the same word or phrase leaves everyone else unmoved. It may not make *sense* but just make a note of them for yourself. One way of learning to handle crumple-buttons assertively is by making them a little less sensitive.

One of the exercises in an assertiveness training class is designed specifically to reduce this sensitivity. If you want to try, you can do this exercise at home with a friend.

First of all, write down two lists; one of valid criticism – that is, things that you know to be true about yourself – and a second list of invalid criticism – labels or epithets which really do not apply to you. Remember the temptation to make everything stick! You will find that this will hinder you making your list of invalid criticisms. You may decide that there is nothing that is not true at *some* time! But it is important to persevere, even with words like dishonest, immoral, dirty, or obviously inappropriate words like domineering, if you know you are very timid, or lazy when you know you work very hard.

When you have written your *two* lists with up to ten words in each, check and see which are your crumple-buttons. When you and your friend have your lists ready, exchange lists, sit facing each other and proceed as follows (I'll give the two women the names Mary and Jane): Mary will alternate valid and invalid criticisms from Jane's list.

Mary: Jane, you're so selfish.
Jane: Yes, I am selfish. It's important to consider my own needs at times.

It is essential to include the actual word – to say 'Yes, I am *selfish*' not just 'Yes, I know I am'. In this way you desensitize the actual word.

Mary gives feedback on how Jane is coming across – on her gestures, her eye contact, her voice, her tone. It is important not to convey apology or defensiveness. They keep repeating the phrase in the same way until both Mary and Jane agree that Jane's reply and manner are really assertive.

Then they proceed to a criticism somewhere on the invalid list.

Mary: Jane, I think you're insensitive.
Jane: That's quite untrue, on the contrary, I am an extremely sensitive person.

It is important that Jane's voice expresses conviction and that she looks at Mary with a steady gaze as she rejects the invalid criticism. It is no good using the words with an apologetic tone or smile. Then Mary goes back to one of Jane's list of valid criticisms. This continues right through to the end of both lists – after which Mary and Jane swap roles and repeat the process with Mary in the 'hot seat'.

This exercise needs about thirty minutes to do effectively (about fifteen minutes each, maybe longer). It is a valuable way of illuminating people's reactions to criticism, and also of identifying the source of much of the resentment and helplessness attached to some of these words. Whether a criticism comes disguised as an outright attack or hidden in a put-down, you may feel there is a grain of truth in it. And you may be interested to know what the other person is trying to tell you. You can use the skill called *negative enquiry*. This helps you to take the initiative. You can ask if there is something critical the other person would like to say to you.

Negative enquiry helps you to prompt criticism in order either to use the information if it turns out that your critic is trying to be constructive, or to expose it if your critic is being purely manipulative or vicious. If it is constructive, you can give the other person an opportunity to express honest, negative feelings which will help to improve communication between you. You are then able to ask and receive criticism from a position of strength. Here are some examples:

Have I behaved insensitively to your feelings?
Are you dissatisfied with the quality of my work?
Do you feel intimidated by me?
Do you think I could have been more supportive?
Do you resent me being successful?
Do you feel rejected by my refusal?
Are you disappointed with the way things have turned out between us?
Do you find me obstinate at times?
Do you feel pushed by me into doing things you don't want?
Are you angry that I'm late?
Are you anxious that I'm going to let you down?

You can also use negative assertion and negative enquiry together. This is a very powerful way of enabling someone to feel secure enough to express negative feelings to you. It also helps you to feel secure enough to listen to what is being said. It does not mean to say you will like what you hear: but at least it can be said directly and there is a chance that the way will be open to a frank and truthful exchange of feelings between you. Here are some examples of how both techniques could be used together:

I find it difficult to handle the question of money. *(negative assertion)* Do you think I'm too aggressive about it? *(negative enquiry)*

I've been very preoccupied lately. *(negative assertion)* Do you find this frustrating? *(negative enquiry)*

I haven't had a lot of sexual experience. *(negative assertion)* Do you find me unsatisfying as a lover? *(negative enquiry – save this for when you're feeling really secure!)*

I've been very tetchy and shouting at you a lot lately. *(negative assertion)* Are you angry at me for not being a more loving mother to you? *(negative enquiry)*

I talk a lot when I'm anxious. *(negative assertion)* Does this irritate you? *(negative enquiry)*

I know I'm inconsistent. *(negative assertion)* Does it drive you up the wall? *(negative enquiry)*

I'm very inquisitive. *(negative assertion)* Do you mind my asking you so many questions? *(negative enquiry)*

If you use the combined skills of negative assertion and negative enquiry you will find that people do not think any the less of you for acknowledging your faults and mistakes. On the contrary, this kind of approach can generate a lot of relief all round. Because you are in a sense *inviting* criticism, it puts you in a much stronger position to handle it. You choose the moment so you are not caught off your guard. Instead of rushing into a panic and responding defensively, you can relax, breathe and listen.

Choose your time wisely to ask the other person. You cannot expect a considered reply if you pounce on someone just as they are rushing through the door or totally preoccupied with something else or once they are already in mid-delivery of a general stream of abuse about you.

The more often you survive hearing something you do not like about yourself, the easier it will be to deal with criticism – both invalid and valid – when they occur unexpectedly. The ability to use these skills will stem from the strength of your own self-esteem. With practice you can hear the criticism without sinking into the 'poor me' Dulcie pattern or rising to the 'Who? Me?' Agnes pattern.

The crucial difference in how you respond will have a lot to do with how you handle your own internal critic. Many of us suffer from listening to the endless critical ramblings of an internal voice which is much more damning than anything we hear from the outside. With or without the help from others, our internal critic can condemn us to the psychic stocks where we sit, waiting passively for the rotten eggs and tomatoes to be thrown in our direction. Somewhere we feel we deserve no better. We feel guilty for what we have done, for who we are and so we stay cramped in the stocks. Although it is possible to get up and walk away, we often feel stuck in position.

It is possible to use criticism wisely – that is, to listen and weigh up for yourself what is said. There is no need to rush around in a panic, making desperate attempts to make yourself into a new and faultless person. Nor need you deafen your ears altogether. There is a lot to be learned from the perceptions of those around us, whatever our relationship with them.

We started this chapter looking at the common experience of criticism as rejection. Being criticized meant being bad and unlovable. We felt helpless in the face of it. Rather than feeling helpless, you can feel strengthened once you understand that it is not the essential *you* that is wrong. It can be a most powerful and enriching experience to receive a criticism clearly and cleanly. In fact, you may not have discovered it yet but criticism can be a *gift*.

Instead of feeling unloved, you can experience criticism as a gesture of regard rather than attack. You can understand that criticism need not stem from someone's low opinion of you – that it can stem from respect or compassion, from a wish to reach out and make contact, from a desire to improve communication and deepen understanding. Criticism can provide a demonstration of someone's clear and loving regard for you as a person in your own right.

Following on

1. Make a list of your own crumple-buttons and try the exercise described in the chapter between Mary and Jane.

2. Just in case you get too immersed in the negative side of your life, give yourself a lift: write down a list of ten positive qualities about yourself. Try not to use words like 'good' but be specific. For example, instead of a good mother use a specific word like loving, patient or affectionate; instead of a good teacher use competent, clear or sympathetic: and instead of a good friend – use loyal, humorous, or understanding.

3. Consider whether you have done or said anything which you suspect upset someone. Is there a general aspect of your behaviour which you think irritates or disappoints or angers someone else? Write down the behaviour and who you feel is affected by it. Write down what you would say to this person if you were to use the skills of negative assertion and negative enquiry.

12

Confrontation and Compliments

Learning to handle criticism when on the receiving end can improve your ability to manage giving criticism to others. This chapter is concerned with the expression of negative feelings to others in a way which allows them to hear what you are saying without feeling attacked or rejected.

How do you express what you consider to be a legitimate grievance or problem you have with someone? How do you express resentment or hurt or disappointment? How do you set about criticizing someone else? Do you avoid direct confrontation altogether like Dulcie, but moan to everyone else *about* the person concerned? Do you go in like Agnes, with a sledgehammer and send the other person reeling away with an ear too thick to hear what you are saying under all the abuse? Or like Ivy, do you make snide remarks, communicating your resentment indirectly, leaving the other person feeling put-down, vaguely guilty without knowing exactly what you are getting at? All these approaches have one thing in common: the message will not be heard either because you have said nothing, or what you have said has been delivered in a way which antagonizes or confuses the other person.

Look more closely at how Ivy, Dulcie and Agnes might behave.

Ivy is under a lot of pressure at work and finds it difficult to cope with the chores at home. She wants to ask her son to help her clear the kitchen.

Ivy comes into the kitchen.

Ivy (in a critical tone):   Look at this mess.

Son (on the defensive):   For heaven's sake, stop moaning.

Ivy (sounding pained):   Well, I'm always the one who has to clear it up.

Son: Nag. Nag. Nag.

Ivy: Don't start being cheeky. If you were more considerate in the first place, I wouldn't have to keep on at you.

Son gets up and walks to the door.

Ivy: Where do you think you're going?

Son: Out. I can't stand this place any more.

Goes out and slams the door.

Ivy is left feeling defeated, resentful and bursts into tears.

Dulcie is a nervous passenger. Her husband is a fast driver and, what's more, prides himself on his driving ability. Every time they go out in the car Dulcie holds on tight, feeling tense and uncomfortable.

Dulcie: Why don't you slow down a bit?

Husband: There's nothing to be frightened of. I know exactly what I'm doing.

Dulcie: Do we have to go this fast?

Husband: It's quite safe. Don't worry.

Dulcie: Why don't you slow down?

Husband: Look, it's all right. *(Impatiently)* I do know what I'm doing, you know. *(Accelerating)*

Dulcie: Yes, but . . .

Husband: Look, close your eyes or something. Leave the driving to me.

He accelerates: Dulcie is too terrified to say any more.

Agnes wants to ask her supervisor for time off the next day. She is discussing this with a colleague when another male colleague says 'Well, you'll just have to wiggle those tits, dear, and I'm sure you'll get your way!'

Agnes (outraged):   You men are all the same. You can't keep your eyes off women's bodies.

Colleague: I can't help but notice, can I?

Agnes: Why don't you piss off?

Colleague: Now don't get nasty. Can't you take a tease?

Agnes: You make me sick,

She walks out, feeling very hurt, humiliated and angry.

Part of the difficulty is that we allow our negative feelings to build up in intensity. Instead of saying something at the time we actually feel the hurt or resentment, we find all sorts of plausible excuses for holding back and keeping quiet. Do you recognize any of the following 'good reasons' for not expressing your feelings?

It's not the right moment? 'We're all having such a lovely time . . . it *is* Christmas after all/I'm in someone else's home/it's the middle of dinner/I can't make a scene in front of these people.'

It's not their fault? 'He's just in a bad mood. She's over-tired/too sensitive or ill or old. She didn't know what she was doing. He can't help it. She just didn't notice. He's going through a bad patch.'

It's not important? 'It's too trivial. I'm being over-sensitive. It's just not worth making a fuss about. I'm not perfect myself.'

Fear of making a bad impression? 'If I'm wrong, I'll look stupid. I don't want to make a fool of myself. I don't want to look petty/unreasonable/ungrateful.'

The need to protect someone else? 'He couldn't take criticism – it would only upset him. She'd feel terribly offended if I told her how I felt.'

Fear of the consequences? 'Maybe he'll criticize *me*/maybe she'll lose her temper. How will they react if I say something *now*, after all this time?'

We get stuck in the compassion trap. We shy away from saying something because we do not want to nag or criticize or make someone feel bad. But, as we have already seen, the resentment and the hurt are shelved – instead of saying something to the person at the time, while it is still fairly small, we store it up, so that eventually the pressure builds up and we explode, often at someone who is close to us and who ends up getting more than their fair share of legitimate criticism.

Suddenly, whether or not someone volunteers to make you a cup of tea becomes a life and death issue. A scratch on the paintwork, the top left off the toothpaste tube, your chair moved slightly out of place, a flippant remark, your last stamp taken without permission, some tiny event can assume huge proportions.

Stored-up resentment distorts what we feel and what we say. We start with an attempt to make a simple statement or request but in the confusion things get out of control, we lose our grip and we grab at anything we know will hit home to help us regain some control of the situation. A small remark escalates to pitched battle with both people fighting it out, making the scene into an *arena*. Here is a sample piece of dialogue you might hear in the arena.

A: That was a stupid thing to do.

B: I wouldn't have done it if you hadn't suggested the idea in the first place.

A: I suggested it because you didn't have any ideas of your own, as usual.

B: Well, the last time I had an idea, you moaned all the way along.

A: Me moan? You didn't stop whining about how crowded it was when we went to the show last week. You never do anything but whine or complain. You're such a drag.

B: Well, you're not exactly hot stuff yourself. Life with you is about as exciting as yesterday's washing up.

A: Oh, so madam's bored is she? Well let me tell you, sweetheart, if it weren't for you, I'd have made something real of my life. . .

Arenas are appropriate for contests – you see the other person as an opponent and one of you has to win. Arenas are fine for having a good fight – they can be exhilarating and stimulating. But they can also be exhausting and a waste of time. The intense feelings will also distort the listener's ability to *hear* what you are saying – they will be too busy running for cover or rising up in challenge. In fact neither person is saying anything much at all – just a lot of generalized vindictiveness. There are many fragments of past hurts and frustrations flying around which make easy weapons – but the clarity gets lost in the exchange of missiles. If it is clear communication that you want, if you want a dialogue, if you want the other person to *listen* to you and understand you, then you will need to establish the more civilized atmosphere of a *forum*. You can use a forum for establishing a climate of mutual respect. You want to say your piece and to listen to the other person. The aim is clear and effective communication.

How can you set up a forum to express negative feelings assertively? If you want to criticize in a way that will encourage the other person to hear what you are saying without scoring points or acting as a self-appointed judge – then the following guidelines will be helpful:

   1. Choose your time and place wisely. If you do this, you will be in a much better position to express yourself clearly. If you want to confront someone, do not wait until it happens again, and kid yourself that *next* time you will say what you really want to. When the next time comes around, the feelings are just as strong, maybe stronger, and you risk making a mess of it again. If you feel at all uncertain about confrontation, give yourself an easier start by setting up the time in advance. A simple statement: 'I'd like to make some time to talk to you about something important' – five minutes, an hour, whatever you want. The other person is then prepared and so are you. This way, you can give yourself a chance to establish a forum climate.

2. Describe the behaviour, do not label the person. Consider the difference between these two statements: 'You're such a bully, always trying to belittle me in front of others' and 'I feel belittled in front of others when you interrupt what I am saying and criticize me for not knowing what I'm talking about.' The first labels the person, and suggests that the effect is intentional. The second simply expresses how you *feel* about the behaviour and the effect it has on you. This can be called assertive confrontation.

3. Express your feelings about the behaviour. This step allows you to state your feelings without putting yourself in a position of dubious authority. None of us likes to be told we are immature or lazy or promiscuous or selfish. It rankles. It reminds us of the labelling in our experience of criticism in the past. The immediate reaction will then be defensive. So state how you *feel*. You have learned how to express and assert your feelings and will remember that no one can argue with how you feel. A straight statement of feeling does not come across as superior so there is more chance that the other person will listen to what you are saying.

It is tempting to use labels. It is tempting to heap the coals of blame on to the other person. Although you may feel temporarily better for getting it all off your chest and watching someone wither under the barrage, remember that ultimately you risk lack of communication.

We tend to assume that we know exactly what someone's intentions are because we know what motivates *us* to say or do the same things. So we say, for example, 'How could she have done that? She must have known it would upset me', or 'He knew how I felt so he obviously did it to annoy me'. Although you *may* be right, there is always the chance that you can be mistaken when you use your own behaviour as a reference point for interpreting everyone else's actions and intentions. It may just be that the other person was not deliberately trying to hurt or attack you.

People do not always know how deeply a remark can hurt or offend you, or how important something is to you. They do not always know what you need or want – maybe you were not clear in the first place. And if you have successfully hidden your feelings in the past, then it can come as quite a shock to the person to know what your true feelings were. Rather than jumping straight in and accusing, you can give them the benefit of the doubt. If, after you have done this, and then knowing quite clearly what offends or hurts you, they repeat it, then you are dealing with a different situation. But first, try stating how you feel about the person's behaviour and letting them know *honestly* how it affects you.

4. Be specific. Ask for a specific change. Constructive criticism in the assertive sense is quite different from a general pronouncement about right or wrong. Simply saying 'you're boring', 'immature', 'stupid' or 'selfish' is not helpful. Even dropping vague hints about wanting more attention or help in the house, for example, is insufficient.

The disadvantage of vague suggestions is two-fold. First, if you do not say exactly what it is you do want then the other person will not know. So how can they agree to do what you ask if they are not clear about what it is they are agreeing to? It also makes it difficult for you if three weeks later you complain, 'Well, I asked you to help me more about the house' and the reply is 'Well, I did wash the cups yesterday'. What do you say? *You* know you meant more than that, but if you did not say so, you have no redress. Being specific is what distinguishes constructive criticism from an attack or complaint. Take responsibility for saying what you want, clearly and directly. Do not assume that the other person is inside your head and will know automatically. Remember, constructive criticism is an equal interaction so you need to be as clear as possible. People are often willing to respond if they are given a clear and specific instruction.

Beware of allowing your attempts at constructive criticism to degenerate into giving unsolicited advice about how other people should behave. Statements like 'You should be more understanding', 'You shouldn't be so sensitive', 'You should be more sociable', 'You should be more ambitious' come across as attacks on someone's personality. The aim is not to cast random judgements on others, however well-meaning, but to state how you feel about one item of behaviour that can be changed.

Consider how Ivy, Dulcie and Agnes could have handled their previous situations with these guidelines in mind:

Ivy: I want to talk to you about helping me in the house.

Son: Oh no, not that again.

Ivy (firmly): I know we've been through it before but I wasn't very clear. Now I'd like to talk to you calmly about it.

Son: What do you want? *(Grudgingly but listening)*

Ivy: I've been under a lot of pressure lately and I just can't cope any more. I get resentful *(feeling)* when you leave all the clearing up to me. *(Son's behaviour)* I'd like you to clear the kitchen once a day. *(Specific change)*

Son: It's not my job to do it.

Ivy: I know it's not your favourite occupation but I need the help. I'd like you to clear the kitchen once a day.

Dulcie approaches her husband while they're at home, *not* driving.

Dulcie: I want you to listen to me. I really feel so terrified when you drive that I'm a wreck by the end of the journey. I would like you to drive more slowly when I'm in the car. *(Specific change)*

Husband: I know what I'm doing.

Dulcie: I realize you know what you're doing, but it terrifies me.

Husband: I didn't realize you were that frightened.

Dulcie: Well, I didn't say so clearly but I just can't stand it. I know it sounds silly but that's what I feel.

Agnes approaches her colleague in advance and sets up a few minutes to talk in private. She does not want to discuss this in full view of everyone because she feels she has a better chance of a clear interaction without anyone else there.

Agnes: I would like you to listen carefully. When you make comments about women's bodies, and my body in particular, I feel hurt and outraged. I find them deeply offensive. I don't know if you are aware of how strongly I feel about them.

Colleague: It's just my sense of humour.

Agnes: It may be funny to you but I find the remarks extremely offensive and I would like to you stop. *(Specific change)*

Each woman has expressed her feelings, described the behaviour and asked for a specific change. The conviction with which you express yourself will depend on the next point.

5. *Spell out the consequences.* This does not have to be a 'do-it-

or-else' threat. In fact you may never have actually to spell out the consequences in so many words but it is very important that you have worked out *for yourself* what the consequences are. These can be positive or negative consequences. It may be easier to express the positive consequences, what will happen if the other person co-operates. Ivy, for example, might feel that a positive consequence of her son's help would be that she would feel less strained and more friendly towards him. The atmosphere in the house would be better. Dulcie might say that she would stop being so tense and irritable and enjoy being with her husband more. Agnes might have said that she would be more willing to co-operate on a working level if her colleague were to stop making personal remarks.

The negative consequences are more problematic. They may be minor or major: a decision to shop elsewhere if service is unsatisfactory or change your doctor if denied proper treatment; or it could mean leaving a relationship. This step is a powerful point of self-confrontation. If you care enough about yourself and the relationship, you will care enough to follow through. Otherwise ask yourself why you are criticizing in the first place. Asking for a change in someone's behaviour and then ignoring the fact that nothing comes of it only undermines you. No one will take you seriously, least of all yourself. This step helps you look at how much you are prepared to put up indefinitely with the existing problem.

If your neighbour refuses to stop bothering you, the only solution may be to leave or move house; if your partner does not stop drinking, the solution may be to move out; if your friend will not stop lying to you, you may have to stop seeing them; if your boss will not give you more money, you may have to change jobs. All these are major steps and ones which you may not want to take. But at least having realized this, you can look at what you will settle for at the moment. Instead of spending your life in a state of agitation, you could spend your energy on other things. If you have taken the trouble to express *exactly* how strongly you feel to the person concerned, you will still feel better when you are not harbouring the resentment inside. Obviously this decision is a very personal one. We have our own individual limits. However much you may look from the outside at someone else's situation and say 'I don't know how you put up with it, I'd have left ages ago', each person will take what they want and decide on their own limits. We move if and when we are ready.

Be gentle with yourself and others: since we handle criticism so badly in our own culture, you need to be sensitive to the impact this sort of confrontation can have. The other person may well regard it as a slap in the face and be rather shocked by your approach so that even though you are being assertive and *not* aggressive, your approach may be misunderstood.

Take an example. Nicole and Debbie are friends. Nicole is pleased to have Debbie to stay but has stored up a lot of resentment that Debbie has not contributed to her keep. Over the weeks, she would have liked her to have bought a little food, taken her out to a meal, offered to pay for something, maybe bought a couple of bottles of wine. She has not actually *said* anything before.

Nicole: Debbie, I've been meaning to say for ages, I'm resentful about your never having paid for anything while you've been staying.

Debbie (shocked): You never mentioned money. I thought I was a guest.

Nicole: Well you are a guest, but you could have bought some wine or paid for something. (1)

Debbie (hurt and defensive): You're saying I'm mean, aren't you? If you'd been staying with *me*. . .

Nicole: I'm not saying you're mean. And I take full responsibility for not saying anything clearly at the time. I should have sorted it out and been direct but I wasn't. I expect you are quite surprised and angry with me. *(Negative enquiry. 2)*

Debbie: Well, I am upset. And yes, I'm cross that you haven't said anything before. It doesn't say much for our friendship if you couldn't be honest with me.

Nicole: You're right. I accept that. I'm sorry.

Debbie: I could always find somewhere else to stay.

Nicole: Well, you don't have to for my sake. I love having you here, you're terrific company and you've been really supportive recently. All I want is for us to come to some arrangement that we both feel happy about.

The key lies in the statements numbered 1 and 2. Number 1 is reproachful. Nicole is not taking responsibility for her own past lack of assertive behaviour but reproving Debbie instead. Number 2 is on the level and *equal*. She accepts responsibility and invites some criticism in return. This is the difference between assertive criticism and one-sided or destructive criticism. The principle of equality remains throughout the interaction – even if you are taking the initiative to confront, you are seeing the other person as equal. You can use this model to talk with the other person rather than saying your piece and running away.

Another hazard to watch for is the *museum*. Sometimes in a relationship which is long-standing, there is a history to it. The psychological museum is full of relics from the past – and not all from the same era. Each section in the musuem represents other periods in our lives and other relationships. But all the rooms contain relics taken from the scene of the time. With remarkable accuracy we remember each incident in detail; the museum houses our unspoken or half-spoken resentments, our unresolved battles. We collect the unforgiven deeds, the offensive remarks as mementoes. They are there to bring out as ammunition to fuel our grievances and grudges. One small event leads to the backlog of a lifetime.

Keeping out of the museum is important. You can still handle your feelings in an important relationship but choose *one thing at a time*. It is too complex to take on a whole relationship at once so start with matters that you can handle.

A final suggestion is to *end on a positive note*. This does not mean ingratiating yourself with the other person: 'Well, I do like you really/and don't take any notice of what I've just been saying/it's really nothing/it's not important.' This means a positive and true statement about how you feel, for example:

'I'm glad to have had this chance to talk to you.'
'I'm relieved to have got that off my chest.'
'I'm grateful to you for listening.'
'I've enjoyed being able to talk about these things with you.'

If appropriate, you can add a positive statement about the other person. Like Nicole appreciating her friend. You can find some remark to balance the interaction, some small positive comment which shows you genuinely value the other person and are not only seeing the negative.

This brings us to an equally important skill.

Giving and Receiving Compliments

Curiously enough, we encounter similar difficulties when handling positive and appreciative comments. We notice things but we refrain from saying anything because we feel inept and uncertain as to how to proceed. And if we do make an attempt, then our efforts are often met with embarrassment and awkwardness – so that we hastily take cover, convinced that it is not worth all the trouble.

If you want to say something appreciative to someone, how do you go about it? Do you ignore it? Do you feel embarrassed giving a compliment and find yourself mumbling something almost inaudibly under your breath or saying something very general, like 'You're great/wonderful/fantastic/terrific' which makes a start in conveying a positive message, but falls short in that such words leave the other person unsure about what exactly you mean?

Overcoming your own awkwardness can be the first hurdle:

> Rita, a forthright woman who had no difficulty expressing her feelings in other ways, found it impossible to tell her teenage daughter that she was impressed by her hard work and achievement at school. She wanted to tell her but didn't know how. With role-play she practised and eventually was able to express to her daughter not only her feelings of awkwardness but also her pride and appreciation.

An assertive expression of appreciation involves a little polish and refinement. Instead of using a vague term like 'great' or 'good', you could be more specific, as in these examples:

> 'That was a very difficult situation – you handled it very sensitively.'
>
> 'I'm impressed by your persistence in such difficult circumstances.'
>
> 'I value the time and trouble you take to make me feel comfortable.'
>
> 'I admire you being so honest even though it was a risk.'
>
> 'You look quite stunning in that outfit.'

Being on the receiving end. Usually, our own embarrassment makes us respond defensively. We dismiss what the other person says in a variety of ways. Can you recognize the following? Someone compliments you on something you're wearing and you quell their enthusiasm with a retort like 'What? *This* old thing?' or you look quite incredulous, 'What do you mean I look elegant in this dress? I bought it ten years ago for sixpence!' If someone praises you for a task well done, your modesty assumes exaggerated proportions and you deny any credit, 'No, no, it was nothing' or even 'Don't make such a fuss about it'.

Quite unintentionally, we manage to ridicule the other person. Our defensive reactions at best make their gesture look inappropriate and at worst, quite stupid. Remember from your own experience, that when someone *does* make the effort to give you a genuine compliment, they could be feeling vulnerable. Another defensive reaction to avoid is the automatic return: no sooner has the compliment left the other person's lips than you are straight in with an immediate and often insincere reply: 'Oh, but *yours* is lovely too' or 'I was *just* thinking the same about you!' This again stems from our anxiety and easily negates whatever the other person has said.

Spot the difference. Have you ever caught yourself thinking 'Now *what* are they after?' when someone gives you a compliment? It is probably because you are suspicious that a compliment is simply flattery and is being used to manipulate you in some way. And you are often right!

'But you did it so *well*,' they say when trying to make you change your mind, and do it again! Or, 'We always felt you were the right kind of person,' they say when trying to persuade you to take on a job that nobody else wants! Or, 'You've always been *so* understanding', you hear as they are about to cheat you out of your fair share. Or, 'You're such a rock,' they say, with a pat on the back when they are too uncomfortable to admit that you are hurt and vulnerable. And, 'I always admire a liberated woman!' as the hand slides further up your thigh!

It is true that compliments are used manipulatively but in our defensivenesss we risk throwing everything out indiscriminately. We learn to distrust compliments of *any* kind. A first step is to identify the duds and handle them in the same way as put-downs (Chapter 11). The second is to learn to receive assertively those which are offered in sincerity.

If you are not sure, ask the person to be clearer. If you are assured that a compliment is sincere, practise a simple acknowledgement – just a smile or 'thank you' is sufficient for the other person to know that their compliment has been received – not dismissed or rejected.

If you are sure that the intention is honourable but are just not clear what is meant by 'amazing' or 'incredible', then again *ask*. Just a gentle encouragement helps the other person to make a little more effort to be specific. That effort can be much more rewarding for both of you.

You may want to go further and agree with the compliment. This does *not* mean an arrogant dismissal, which implies that the speaker is stating something *so* obvious, that she/he need not have bothered. It means simply agreeing with what the other person says:

'Thank you. I like this colour on me too.'
'I'm glad you like it. I think it suits me better this way.'
'I'm reassured that you think so. I wasn't sure if I'd done the right thing or not.'
'I'm pleased you noticed. I was quite proud of myself as well!'

Any comment that comes naturally to you that allows you to show that you have heard what was said and that you liked it.

Small and simple, spontaneous and specific. The danger with looking at compliments in this way is that you will feel even more embarrassed and self-conscious than before. It is important to practise. It then becomes easier and you can allow yourself to be more spontaneous.

One difference between handling criticism and compliments is that the strength of the negative feelings will usually emerge somehow – aggressively or indirectly – but all too often the positive feelings become submerged. We forget to say to people we love that we love them – we use elaborate expensive cards with flowery words instead of using simple words of our own. We can say thank you for tangible presents at Christmas, maybe, but we forget to say thank you on all those small but numerous occasions which do not merit a big production but which could easily be honoured with a simple word of appreciation.

One final point is that, with experience, you will be less afraid to speak out and express appreciation simply because you feel like it. You will find it easier to respond immediately to people. We become so stuck in habits of comparison and competition that we forget how to reach out simply with a little word or gesture of love or praise or acknowledgement just for the sake of it. A spontaneous hand-out that is sincere, heartfelt and absolutely free.

13

An Assertive Approach
to Work and Money

Most women work. This chapter concerns not only women who are in paid employment, but those women who spend a lot of their time cleaning, cooking and caring for their husbands and families. Housework and childcare is often strenuous and demanding labour, even if it is not recognized as official employment.

Whether single or married, with or without a family, working to make a living, to make ends meet or to retain a measure of independence, whether established in a career or returning to work after bringing up a family, it seems that there is some common ground in the difficulties we encounter as working women.

A major obstacle to being assertive at work is the problem of establishing the limits of the job and your particular responsibilities. What are you expected to do? Do you feel you are asked to do more than you are paid to do? What do you demand of yourself? Most of us do not take the time to ask ourselves these questions and, as a result, we get into the habit of taking on more than we want to, and stretching ourselves to the limit.

Joan, a doctor in her forties, shared a busy general practice. She also did everything in the home. She could not ask her husband to help because he had been ill: she did not ask her teenage children to help because they had their own lives to lead. Her elderly father lived with them and needed special attention and since he was *her* father, she felt that the responsibility was hers alone. Even the cat was sick! She raced from one appointment to another, unable to say no to patients, to colleagues, to husband, to her children, to her father, or to the cat. In class, we suggested, 'Why not ask x or y to do this or that?', but she would only insist that it was *her* job. She was managing to do it all, on the surface, but minor family crises quickly became major catastrophes: she snapped at her children, she withdrew from her husband sexually as she was tired, yet each morning she would be up early and she would be on the frenetic treadmill all over again.

Joan is a special example but many women tread similar paths, in that we find it difficult to know where to set limits. Perhaps you know of a woman like Joan. Or are you like her yourself? She illustrates very clearly what can happen when we believe ourselves to be inexhaustible.

'I'll prove I can do it and go on for ever and ever.' If you are a slave to this myth you may find yourself thinking one or more of the following: 'being tired is a sign of weakness or at least admitting I am tired is a sign of weakness', 'I have to muster that last bit of energy from somewhere', 'I have to keep going to the bitter end'. With these thoughts buzzing around, we end up becoming overburdened and depressed, sometimes physically ill. We behave as if we possessed an inexhaustible supply of love and care for others, as if our energy and time and our resources were unlimited!

It can be very difficult to remember that we have the right to acknowledge our own needs for care. It goes against the grain to admit openly that we need to rest and replenish our resources. The urge to prove oneself a tireless superwoman drives us on and on and on. Taking on extra work, working too late at night or at weekends, being ever accessible to clients and patients and family, coping with every crisis around you, anticipating everyone's needs, your mind on a-hundred-and-one things at the same time, all these pressures take their toll eventually – physically, mentally or both.

How do we express this exhaustion? Dulcie is always tired. Her shoulders are hunched, her feet move slowly. She punishes her body by going on too long. Her back aches. She may go and ask the doctor for something to keep her going. She may cry every now and again, with exhaustion. Others may know something is wrong and may even beg her to take a rest but she will not.

Agnes pushes herself hard as well. She rushes around, impatient with anyone who slows her down or does not do what they are supposed to do. She tears around, staying up all night, shouting at others who get in her way, blaming them angrily because they appear to be idling away their time with nothing to do.

Ivy, as you might expect, expresses her feelings indirectly. She too is likely to feel resentful about being put upon but will use guilt to make this known. She may even go out of her way to make some elaborate but quite unnecessary effort, imposing unsolicited care and attention on those around her. They may protest in vain – they don't know whether to feel grateful or guilty but they certainly feel uncomfortable.

An assertive approach starts with realizing how hard it is to break the habit. It is very difficult to get out of what can become a vicious circle: the more tired you become, the more unassertive you feel and therefore feel less able to set limits and say enough is enough. Instead of calling a halt when you need most to do so, you can find yourself believing that just a little bit more cannot make *that* much difference.

Many women begin to see this as an addiction: there is a lot of pleasure and satisfaction to be found in stretching yourself to achieve fifty goals where anyone else would only have achieved ten. And there is a curious pride we can feel in achieving what others assume impossible.

Breaking out of the circle needs to be done very gradually. Selma decided to start in a small way in her own life. Setting aside half an hour each day was a beginning – just to do whatever she wanted – lie down, sit, walk, rest, whatever. It takes a mammoth effort of will because she can still find thirty things she 'should' be doing but she manages to allow the guilt to hover without giving in to it. If the phone rings or the children knock at the door, she reminds them that this is *her* time. She needs the time to review how she can begin to 'prune' her other activities: where she can begin to cut back, ask for help and say 'no' to more.

This is what Dorothy had to do. She worked as a nurse at night in a local hospital: childcare and housework took care of the rest of her day – allowing herself virtually no rest and little sleep. She knew she was too tired but what she needed to do was first acknowledge her *need* to ask for help from her husband and then to see how she could get that help. By asking her husband to do some shopping and her sister to pick up the children from school, she was able to make a start.

Making the first step is difficult. You first need to recognize yourself when things have gone too far. It is easy to pretend that you can still manage and that things have not really got out of hand at all. It can creep up on you! Deidre had been working for two years as a secretary and P.A. to a busy executive. Almost unnoticeably, her job, which had started as eight hours a day, had taken over her evenings and most of her weekends. The more competent she proved herself to be, the more her boss asked her to do, or assumed that she would do and of course, she did. She did not once say 'no', but just let everything build up more and more until she found she had no time for personal life at all. Looking at why she always allowed herself to take on more and more, she realized that she did not want to say 'no' because she feared appearing unwilling, uncommitted, unco-operative, so she failed to set clear limits with her boss. She decided at this point that she needed to look at ways in which she could ensure sufficient personal free time while still coping with her job. For her, this meant approaching her boss and exploring the situation together.

Sandra fell into a similar pattern. She worked as a sub-editor on a magazine and always found herself the one to be asked to take home manuscripts at weekends. She wanted to say 'no' but also wanted to be obliging. Practising saying 'no' and negotiating a workable compromise were useful to her.

Being amenable, friendly, committed and above all obliging may be important aspects of the image you want to project to others. But sometimes the expectation becomes a trap. You become known as obliging – people rely on you to be obliging, you can always be depended on to say 'yes' where someone else would say 'no'. This makes it increasingly difficult to begin changing the pattern. The first time you say 'no', your uncharacteristic response may cause a little consternation and this is often the crunch point: 'But you usually/but you always/but we've been able to depend on you in the past. . .' they will say. Once you get over this hurdle, it gets easier. It helps to be able to practise saying 'no' first in a role-play situation. You can then feel more comfortable with it before making the decision to apply it in real life. Just being able to experience *once* a way of doing it differently is an important beginning.

Judy found this to be true for her. As a single teacher she found herself constantly lumbered with various duties after school or on Saturdays, even taking children away in the holidays. The staff assumed that she would oblige, which of course she did. She felt she did not have the right to say 'no', as she did not have family responsibilities like the others. Once Judy admitted that she did not want to take on all that extra work, she was able to exercise more discretion. She learned to define more clearly her dual obligation to herself and her colleagues and from that position could then choose to give up *some* of her free time after school hours, but not all of it.

The boundaries between personal and working life can become

blurred in other ways. Sometimes our rights to privacy are over-looked.

Lucy arrived one evening in great distress. After ten years' absence from paid work, having a family, she had started a job as a clerk in an insurance office. The personnel manager had called her in to say that he was going to contact her family doctor to find out details of her past medical history. She was so stunned when he said this that she said nothing. In fact, she was anxious that the personnel department should not delve into her past – she had been in hospital twice for depression and suspected that this would be held against her. With the group's support and encouragement, she went in to work the next day and made an appointment to see the personnel manager. She told him assertively that she didn't want him to write to her doctor as she felt this to be an infringement of her privacy. She felt that she was taking a risk that she might lose the job in doing so, but her wishes were respected on this occasion without any negative consequences.

Glynis was particularly unhappy about two women in the factory where she worked, who persisted in asking her all about her private life. Where was she going in the evening? What had she done at the weekend? Who was she seeing? Who was the man who had met her from work last week? And so on. She did not know how to handle it. When she role-played it in the group, she found that several other women found it difficult to refuse to answer similar direct questions. It took practice but Glynis was eventually able to convince them without being hostile that she did not want to answer their questions.

Barbara experienced a different kind of confusion. She found that she could not make the boundaries sufficiently clear between her own personal and professional life. At work, she was a student counsellor: her ability to listen, her sympathetic manner were very evident. But her problem was that some of her friends also found in her a good listener and she would find herself listening to troubles by night as well as by day. She found it difficult to acknowledge her resentment to herself and then to admit directly to her friends that she wanted to be herself in her free time and talk about her own life as well.

Working as a woman in a man's world poses different problems. Alice was a sales manager, the only woman in an area where all the other seven managers were men. Once a month they had an area meeting and tea would be brought in during the afternoon. Every month, the tray was pushed round the table to Alice who would pour out the tea and pass around the cups seething silently inside!

How would Dulcie have dealt with the situation? She would probably have continued to pour the tea and resigned herself to the fact that it was her role. What did it matter anyway, pouring out a few cups of tea? Men were such babies. Wherever they were, they still needed someone to play mother!

Agnes would have poured the tea for a while and then, suddenly and without warning, might stand up and say 'Who the hell do you think I am? I'm not here to wait on you. Get your own bloody tea!', leaving uncomfortable silences, embarrassment and little room for communication.

Ivy might have masked her aggression. Or she may have poured her own tea and then avoided the glances of the others while she sipped her own tea, not saying a word, but getting her message across in her own particular way.

What Alice practised in class was to call for the attention of the group and confront them assertively: month after month, she had been asked to pour the tea and she felt this was an unfair assumption that, as she was the only woman present, this should be her task. She was prepared to pour the tea this time, but only if they could agree that each person took a turn each month. In this way, her next turn would be in eight months' time. With practice, she was able to say all this without her accumulated resentment spilling out in her manner and voice. She decided to try it out on the next occasion and was pleased with the result.

Sexual Harassment

Another way in which many women experience someone over-stepping the boundaries between personal and professional spheres is with sexual harassment. Sometimes the harassment is quite obvious. Ruth worked as a waitress in a busy restaurant at lunch-time. One man, a regular, and a good customer, would always catch her attention by pinching her thigh or her bottom as she walked by. This made her angrier and angrier until, one lunchtime, she could not stand it any longer, and really let go at him. She lost her job.

Or the harassment may involve a more subtly patronizing approach. Rosie was called in to her boss as part of the monthly review in the department. She was told she needed to produce more material and although her work was good, she needed to pull her weight a bit more. She did not enjoy the criticism but accepted it and knew it was valid. Later that day, before going home, her boss came into the room where she was working. He suddenly announced that he had been a bit hard on her and could he make it up by taking her out to dinner that evening. She was appalled and horrified. Suddenly she felt no longer treated as an employee, capable of receiving criticism – just as a potential sexual object. But she did not know what to do. She did not accept the invitation but swallowed her resentment and humiliation because she did not know how to handle it.

Elena, who was gay and openly so at work, was subjected to constant harassment by a particular male colleague who would always manage to interject some remark about her sexual activity with a lascivious tone. Whenever she tried to object, she would be told that she was simply being defensive and anti-male. With practice she was able to confront him effectively so that he could understand just how offensive his behaviour was to her.

Sexual harassment is very much in the news. It is easy to do a Dulcie or Agnes but either way, the message that such behaviour can be extremely offensive does not always get home. Women often share the experience of feeling both humiliation and rage and are not quite sure how to handle either.

The guidelines given earlier about the expression of feelings (see page 64) can be usefully applied here:

1. Trust your perception. The first and in some ways the worst hurdle to clear is the moment when you realize that it is actually happening to *you*. At this point, we may feel disgust, outrage and incomprehension, feelings which are intensified by associated experiences in the past, especially childhood. At the same time, we are paralysed by panic. And it is usually this fear and a sense of shame that prevent us from taking immediate action.

If you do not recognize what you feel, you may well let it go in favour of some kind of rationalization: 'This is not really happening to me: I'm imagining it. His hand must have slipped. After all, the train is *very* crowded.' We make excuses for the other person and hold back from reacting by persuading ourselves that with a bit of luck, it will stop. Learning to trust in your immediate response has been discussed as important to assertive behaviour in all sorts of settings – in this one, it is vital.

2. Once you have managed to do this, the next step will depend on the context. In a public place, for example, a crowded train or bus, cinema or park you may be well advised to try a strong verbal rebuff. Something simple and to the point like 'Stop it!', particularly

if the harassment is physical. You may need to practise getting the right note (see Chapter 10) or you may decide that if you are being touched up by someone sitting next to you, a quick, sharp hard pinch on the thigh would be more immediately effective. There are several classes at the moment which are designed to teach women how to defend themselves from physical attack.

3. If the harassment is more subtle or occurs at work, then you need a different approach. The main obstacles to assertive confrontation in these situations appear to be a combination of self-doubt and realistic anxiety about the consequences of losing your job, being left unsupported or ostracized by your colleagues. You may need to find yourself some reinforcement. See if there are any colleagues at work whom you can trust to give you the support you need. The confrontation skills outlined in Chapter 12 can be used here. It will also help to practise them with a friend or at home beforehand. It is important to state how you feel and to let the person know how their behaviour or attitude affects you. If you manage a confrontation assertively once, you will build up your confidence and you will probably find that you can deal more easily with the one-off harassments to which, as women, we risk continual subjection.

Money

Sometimes, as women, we experience harassment in the form of sexist put-downs. Ever since a male client said quite seriously, when I stated my professional fee, 'You charge a lot for a woman', I have been pondering the complexity of the issues surrounding women and money. Although not everyone works for money, it is impossible to avoid the subject altogether. And since our feelings about and attitudes towards money often prevent assertive behaviour, it seems appropriate to look at some of the problems in this chapter.

Money is powerful. Economic inequality between men and women is a major factor involved in women's attitude to money. Many women are frustrated by a financial structure of wealth and opportunity which continues to favour men over women, giving men more financial power. Some women shun money as a tool of a capitalist and male system and therefore something to be avoided. They believe that no woman should charge another woman money for anything, as it simply repeats the exploitation of women. Other women want to have money of their own to live within the system, to feel some independence, to have something of their own. For some women this is a reason to work. Money spells freedom. Perhaps freedom from a domestic situation where they are tied with children and to the money brought in by their husband. Many women feel they cannot make a move away from the family without first having money of their own.

We are hidebound by the attitude that it is not feminine to know about, to talk about or to argue about money – a vestige of the traditional belief that men were concerned with money making and money spending. Although women financiers and stockbrokers are increasing, they are still a minority. So at the root of much unassertive behaviour is the belief that it is still not 'nice'. It is embarrassing, unpleasant to talk or think about money. This belief finds its way into many situations.

Maureen found it difficult to query a bill. She would always feel embarrassed and if ever she suspected she was being overcharged in a shop or restaurant, or even if she were short-changed on the bus, she still did not mention it because she was embarrassed to do so.

Jo had planned to go on holiday with Virginia for two weeks. As the time approached, she realized that Virginia, who had a well-paid job, had a lot more money to spend than she did. Jo didn't want to cause an 'atmosphere' between them before they went away, but neither did she want to spoil her holiday worrying.

Kathleen, too, needed some financial help. Her pension was very limited and she knew her daughter would be able and probably only too willing to help her but she felt it was undignified to talk about such things.

Margaret found it extremely difficult to ask for the return of three pounds which she had lent her next-door neighbour. It bothered her whenever she saw the woman and yet she felt too uncomfortable to ask directly. She told herself that she was being too petty and that three pounds shouldn't matter that much. She kept hoping that her neighbour would remember and suddenly produce it. When she did mention it, after practising in a class situation, she found her neighbour had forgotten completely and immediately repaid the loan.

How much are you worth? The discomfort felt when talking about money combined with a lack of self-esteem and self-assertion can present women with many difficulties in negotiating a price for their labours.

If you have to cost your labour, how do you arrive at a price? Do you pick a figure out of a hat? Do you settle on a price that you know is appropriate but then ask for less, get less and moan about all those people charging more than you and getting away with it?

If you do not want to ask for money for whatever reason, are you comfortable with giving away your time and talent or are you selling yourself short? Pam was faced with a dilemma – she had been a hairdresser before she married and enjoyed cutting hair for the women on the estate. But they were friends and did not have much money to spare. An assertive compromise for her was to exchange cutting hair for babysitting time – which suited everyone. She was happy that her time and talent were valued and her customers, who could not afford to pay in cash, were happy to pay in kind.

Lindy made her living as a freelance dressmaker. She found it impossible to set adequate fees, even when she was working for fashion houses who could afford to pay her more than she asked. When she role-played asking her fees, what emerged was her embarrassment at actually mentioning a price directly. It was important for her to practise and practise saying what she wanted as an hourly rate. The anticipation of disapproval comes from within and it is useful to take the time to feel more comfortable with actually stating the fee and sticking to it without falling prey to the various comments that may come back (Chapter 4).

Another trap into which we fall unawares is the conviction that love and money are incompatible: in other words, if you care, you cannot charge money for what you do. This is very strongly endorsed in our culture. We were recently treated to another bout of it in the newspapers concerning nurses' pay. 'If we pay more, we'll get the wrong sort of person attracted to the profession', read the headlines. What does this imply other than if you are committed, devoted, loving and the right sort of person, then you will not want to be bothered with nasty little matters like an adequate wage. Many women struggle with this belief. An assertive approach does not mean being compelled to earn high wages necessarily but it can mean learning the difference between an assertive or passive decision. Choosing a compromise that is purely financial is one thing; compromising your self-respect is another.

This same discomfort with the mention of money causes anxiety in interviews. This can lead us to skip over discussions too casually so that it appears that we are not really concerned about money. Lorna knew she had an important interview coming up and was particularly worried about handling the matter of her salary. We practised the interview in the class, but it emerged that it was important for her to do some background research beforehand. She phoned around and took advice as to what would be a reasonable sum to ask for and what she could expect as a minimum and maximum. Thus prepared, Lorna felt much more confident in coping with those questions at her interview.

Doing your homework is an important aspect of an assertive approach to money. Informing yourself of your rights about taxation or about savings for example can be crucial. Even saving a little out of the family allowance each week, as a woman financial adviser told me, means that many women can put something by to have for themselves. Maria needed to seek advice. She was a single parent and found it very difficult to manage financially. The worry was making her ill, but she did not want to approach the father of her child, as she did not want to be involved with him any further. Before she could practise making an assertive approach, she needed to seek advice as to her financial rights in that situation.

Seeking specialist help and advice in areas where you feel inadequately informed is an important part of assertiveness. Acquiring skills which are job-related also comes into this category. Today there are courses which help women develop their career potential: assertive skills applied to specific management and industrial settings. Women want to learn to use their authority more effectively, to handle conflict and negotiation, to build co-operation and to project themselves more successfully.

But even in a professional context, the basis remains a personal one – knowing and affirming yourself, setting clear limits on your time and energy, having the courage to defend your priorities and values – above all, taking pride in the person that you are.

Following on

1. If you are anticipating an interview for a job, set up a role-play. Give the 'interviewer' some clues as to what to ask.

2. With someone taking the role of a nosy colleague, practise using and repeating the statement, 'I don't want to answer your question.'

3. Talk to your partner about a money concern.

4. Write a personal advertisement for yourself: a job description which sells you and your talents. Put a price to your skills, and afterwards, talk about the experience with someone.

5. Imagine yourself in any of the following situations and practise negotiating a price which leaves you feeling neither guilty nor cheated:

a) For the past two months, you have been giving someone a lift to work. You do not have to go out of your way and you enjoy the company but you want to ask for a contribution to the petrol.

b) Your friends know you cook well. You are asked to cater for a large party. Even though you enjoy cooking, you are aware of all the work involved and would like to ask for some payment, over and above the cost of the food.

c) You are a professional illustrator and a friend asks you, as a favour, to design a special birthday card. He expects you to do it for nothing as it is such a small job. You want to negotiate some payment.

6. Starting with the phrase 'I have to . . .' write down the list of responsibilities you have in your life. When you come to the end, write down 'I choose to . . .' and then copy down the list. See if there is anything you feel responsible for, which you could give to someone else.

7. Make a list of positive qualities you bring to your work. It is easy for women to minimize qualifications and achievement. Practise asserting your strengths and successes out loud to someone in a role-play situation.

14

Your Body – Stranger or Friend?

All too often, a woman's relationship with her body is one of struggle – a conflict between body and mind, appetites and excess, between feelings and reason, pleasure and punishment.

Many women see their bodies if not as an out-and-out enemy, then certainly with the unfamiliarity of a stranger. We are suspicious and uncertain as to how our bodies might respond. We try everything to keep them under control – disguise them, punish them, stuff them, starve them, decorate them, mutilate them, hide them, restrict them, deprive them. We use them to attract, seduce, satisfy, console, give birth and serve others. If they slow down with overwork or old age, we show little respect or sympathy: we push them to their limits or discard them as useless and unattractive, no longer worth any love and attention.

An assertive attitude to your body means learning to understand it, to trust it, to care for it. It especially means learning to live with your body in harmony rather than fighting against it.

In the last chapter we looked at the question of tiredness and saw how we often fail to heed signs of fatigue in our bodies. These signs will vary with each individual but they are clear – your skin comes up in a rash, your stomach may tighten giving you indigestion, your back may twinge or your legs ache. You find yourself having less and less energy. If we detect and follow the signs in good time, we can prevent ourselves overstretching our physical and psychological resources. The chapter on feelings also showed the importance of listening to your body cues instead of ignoring them. Going against your body means attempting to deny to yourself what you feel and want or need – going with your body means accepting the need to express those feelings in some way. Going with your body means taking the time to see what you really need instead of fighting it and turning to food or drink as a means of denial or temporary relief. Listening more carefully to what your body is saying puts you much more in command of your life.

This involves learning about your body. It does not have to be a complete biology course but there are many books (some mentioned at the end of this book) which can help you discover how your body works. Women's health is also the focus of many self-help groups and evening classes. Learning how your body works leads to learning how to care for your body in health. It means taking charge of your body and what you put into it.

Finding out what suits *you* is important. There is no point following tedious or expensive diets and punishing yourself unnecessarily. Monitoring what you put in your body means knowing how to restore the balance: too much of one thing means you need to take in a little more of something else. See how your appetite changes with your moods; how it varies with the pattern of hormonal changes in your body, such as your menstrual cycle. Learning what is good for your body and bad for your body need not be expensive or time-consuming. Once you start thinking about your body as your responsibility, it is easy to notice how you are treating it and what you can change.

This also includes repairing the wear and tear caused by the stress of most of our lives. We live in a state of tension and anxiety a lot of the time, more than we realize. We flake out in the evening and seem to be constantly sighing with tiredness and moaning about another day, wondering if we will ever have the stamina to get through. Making time to rest is important and learning how to relax is vital. Rest may take more organization of the way you spend your time – relaxation can take as little as five minutes but makes a remarkable difference. Find out what relaxes you: walking, meditating, gardening, yoga. Learning to breathe and relax in the middle of a tense and important meeting, discussion or journey helps to reduce the stress and strain on your body. Breathing deeply at any time helps.

How do you exercise your body in a way that you can enjoy? Going for a walk, running, swimming, dancing, not with any goals, but simply to enjoy the exertion and movement, can be part of your daily programme. What are some of the ways in which you could make more time for this in your life? Remember it is no good setting your goals too high because you will never begin to face the difficulty of reorganizing your life. Start small. Taking five minutes a day to do some sort of exercise is a *possible* goal and therefore one which you can reach.

Understanding how to care for your body in health will help you care for your body in sickness. You may be able to do a lot for yourself by understanding why your body is sick. On the other hand if it is beyond your personal knowledge, then you will be much better prepared to handle yourself assertively when you need the expertise of members of the medical profession. What distinguishes an assertive patient from any other is basically her attitude to her body and consequently to the medical specialist she has to deal with.

Dulcie as a patient is likely to swallow anything the doctor gives her and faced with an important decision, about surgery for example, finds it difficult to stand up for her rights. She will end up taking the expert advice because 'they' know best regardless of what she feels or wants in herself.

Agnes is likely to behave passively for a while but her anxiety flares up and often alienates the specialists by telling them their jobs, interfering, and blaming them for everything that goes wrong.

Ivy will often agree with a diagnosis and treatment on the outside but manage to forget the appointment, throw away the tablets and will indirectly sabotage the treatment by never following it through to the end. This quiet way of rebelling is one facet of her desire to take control.

Selma's attitude, however, is based on her attitude to her own body. She feels her body is *hers*. She is familiar with it and knows how it works when well. When something is wrong she uses her doctor as a consultant as she would with anyone with expert knowledge in a particular field: when she wants legal advice, she asks a lawyer; when she wants the brakes on her car fixed, she asks a mechanic. So when she wants to know what is wrong or what to do with her body, she consults her doctor. She does not want to tell the doctor his/her job but nevertheless feels she has the right to ask for information and decide on a course of action in co-operation with the doctor.

It is true that some doctors hold tightly to the principle that a little knowledge is a bad thing and discourage self-help and an assertive approach, preferring to keep the expertise and the power where it is, within the boundaries of the medical profession. But fortunately there are many other doctors who are only too delighted to encourage their patients to take responsibility for themselves. They are happy to give clear, straightforward information and to consider genuinely the needs and interests of the patient.

An assertive attitude as a patient will only work if you have already established an assertive approach to your body. If you go part way to finding out yourself and taking responsibility for your *health*, you can take some responsibility for your body when it is not healthy. A confidence that is rooted in familiarity and care helps to counter the feelings of embarrassment, ignorance and power-lessness that many women experience when in the role of patient. Instead of handing over the power of our bodies easily, as we do, we can make some choices about how we want to be treated. We can use the advice and knowledge of the experts and still take more responsibility for ourselves.

One final way of building a more assertive approach to our bodies is by giving ourselves more pleasure. We usually see our lives as ninety per cent effort and toil with pleasure confined to the other ten per cent. We tend to think of pleasure as something to be indulged in occasionally – when we are rich or have nothing better to do, like on holiday. Pleasure can be an occasional treat but even then we manage to feel guilty about it. Have you ever found yourself justifying a holiday on the grounds of how long it is since you last had one or how hard you have been working or how inexpensive this particular deal turned out to be?

Pleasure need not be the sole possession of the so-called idle rich. It is everywhere. If you find this difficult to believe you will learn from Exercise 2 at the end of this chapter. It is an exercise on simple sensual pleasures: you can discover that there is a lot around simply for the noticing; that pleasure is already part of your daily life and that it does not necessarily cost money.

Taking the time to give yourself a little conscious pleasure helps counteract the idea that your body is just a workhorse or ornament. If you can give yourself permission to enjoy pleasure you will be better able to allow others to give you pleasure which is one of the aspects of the next chapter on sexuality.

Saying 'no' and 'yes' for your body means saying 'no' and 'yes' for yourself. Having learned the truth of this, many women who attend an assertiveness training class take steps to say 'no' and 'yes' for their bodies, seeing it as an important statement of doing something for themselves: saying 'no' to cigarettes, saying 'no' to intercourse when you do not want it, saying 'no' to extra work when you are tired, saying 'no' to eating all the children's leftovers, saying 'no' to swallowing back tears, saying 'yes' to bicycling, saying 'yes' to an extravagant box of chocolates, saying 'yes' to a long scented bath, saying 'yes' to an extra hour in bed, saying 'yes' to sexual pleasure, saying 'yes' to a weekly swim, saying 'yes' to buying yourself a bunch of flowers, saying 'yes' to the offer of a lift when you are tired, saying 'no' to the offer of a lift when you need the exercise. Some women even found themselves losing weight throughout the course and one even reported an extra half-inch in height! Look at ways in which you can say 'yes' and 'no' for your body and yourself in your own life.

Information, familiarity, care, pleasure: it sounds like being a friend to your body, which it is. It is important to respect, cherish and care for your body, for yourself. Finding how we function in our bodies can help us find out how we function as people. We *are* our bodies after all, but we tend to lose this unity. Regaining it as far as possible is a great step forward.

Following on

1. Use the ideas in the chapter to find three things in your life you could say 'no' or 'yes' to for yourself. Remember to start with small goals.

2. *Pleasure exercise.* Take a large piece of paper and write down, on the left-hand side, a list of twenty pleasures – these can be very simple. Here are some examples: the taste of chocolates, the sound of the wind, the smell of a rose, an absorbing book, laughing with a close friend, sunshine on your back, the smell of the sea, dancing, holding the hand of a small child, a long hot bath, a cat curled up on your lap, the smell of warm bread, strawberries, a sunset, an open fire, clean sheets, singing when you are by yourself, the feeling of peace when everyone has gone to bed, holding a baby, a favourite piece of music, a cuddle, frying bacon, having your hair washed.

When you have written down at least twenty, the next step is to divide the rest of the page into three columns. In the first column put a T or an A which stand for Together or Alone. This means whether you enjoy the pleasure on your own, or whether you need someone else to enjoy it with. If it is a pleasure which can be enjoyed alone *or* together with someone, put T/A. In the second column put a £ sign – a large £ indicates an expensive pleasure, a small £ sign indicates that the pleasure costs a little money. In the last column, write down how long it is since you enjoyed that particular pleasure. This does not need to be precise – just an idea of whether it is hours, days, weeks or months. Then take the time to see what your list says about your approach to pleasure. Are there opportunities all around you in your everyday life? Are there some things you have not enjoyed for a long time with no good reason? Do you have more pleasure alone or with another person? Do all your pleasures cost money? What do you learn about yourself?

3. *Relaxation exercise.* This is a short but effective exercise adapted from the *The Assertive Woman*. Make sure you are in a quiet place either lying down on a bed or the floor or sitting comfortably in a reclining chair. Following these instructions you create and relieve tension in the muscles through your body. Get a friend to read the instructions at first or record them yourself on a cassette.

Tense and relax each part of your body *three* times.

a) Make an exaggerated frown and then stretch your eyebrows up to your hairline. Relax.

b) Close your eyes as tightly as you can for five seconds. Relax.

c) Draw the corners of your mouth back and stretch for five seconds. Relax.

d) Clench and then loosen your jaw.

e) Stretch your arms in front of you. Clench fists tightly for five seconds. Relax.

f) Push your arms out against an invisible wall and push forward with hands for five seconds. Relax.

g) Bend your elbows. Tense your biceps for five seconds. Relax.

h) Shrug your shoulders up to your ears for five seconds. Relax.

i) Arch your back off the floor or bed for five seconds. Relax. Feel the anxiety and tension disappearing.

j) Hold in your abdomen as tight as you can for five seconds. Relax.

k) Imagine you have got a £5 note in between your buttocks. Then imagine holding on to it while someone else is trying to pull it away! Relax.

l) Tighten thigh muscles by pressing legs together as tightly as you can for five seconds. Relax.

m) Tighten your knees and calves for five seconds. Relax.

n) Bend ankles towards your body as far as you can, for five seconds. Relax.

o) Point your feet away from you. Relax.

p) Curl your toes under as tightly as you can for five seconds.

Relax.

Take a further minute to stay breathing calmly, feeling your body relaxed.

15

Sexuality and Assertiveness

Sex, sex, sex . . . newspapers titillate our Sundays with it, advertisers exploit it, magazines urge us to be better at it, books are banned because they say too much about it, films and television plays are censored if they show too much of it. We talk about it in secretive exchanges, hushed tones or poke fun at it with bawdy laughter. There are a lot of people at the moment wanting to help people who have got problems with it.

We seem to have a variety of general pictures of sex in our culture. One is of some untamed monster that has to be kept under the tightest control through fear of the untold havoc that would be caused if it were to be unleashed. So it is better left alone, not talked about, hidden, denied, repressed and remaining a dark presence lurking in the cellar somewhere. The difficulty with this image is that the very thought of it is enough to send our pulses racing in anxiety and panic.

A second image is of a complex piece of electronic machinery. This image stems from a preoccupation with the mechanics of sexual performance. Researchers examine sexual behaviour in minute detail until everything is catalogued and labelled and fitted into neat little categories. This image of sex confuses us too. It seems to imply that sex is only a matter of how often who puts what where, and leaves us feeling inadequate. But many people feel there is a lot more to it than that: like love, warmth, celebration and pleasure. Sex is one of the important ways we can communicate with another person through our bodies. A loving embrace can afford us relief from tension, reassurance and a feeling of physical and emotional well-being. But these positive aspects of human sexuality suffer from under-exposure. Instead, we are caught up in the cultural pressures: towards restraint and anxious silence or towards goals of sexual achievement. The guilt, the ignorance and general discomfort with attempts at honest communication about sexual matters filter through to the way in which many women regard their own sexual behaviour. These attitudes emerge time and time again as underlying difficulties in the problems of communicating clearly with sexual partners. Some of these attitudes are expressed in the following myths. Have you ever expressed these statements or thought them to yourself?

'**Sex is a waste of time.**' Many women feel there is absolutely nothing in it for them at all. Or it can be regarded as the first thing to go when other things call – children, work, endless tasks which take priority over something as frivolous as sexual pleasure. This can be due to consistently unsatisfactory sexual experience and no means of dealing with it. Consider what importance sex has for you. Is time spent being sexual with someone personally rewarding or is it about as exciting as the occasional sneeze? Has it become just another daily chore or routine?

'**It doesn't look good to know too much about "it".**' Better play innocent and ignorant. Less bother that way and less responsibility. Do you make time, take time to find out, to read about sexual matters? Are you interested enough to enquire, to find out, to explore? Nowadays women are beginning to read more and some are taking the brave step of attending special groups and courses concerned with female sexuality as one way of exploring and discovering for themselves.

'**I'd be lost without you.**' The difficulty with this belief is two-fold. Many women feel that when they do not have a partner, they are automatically unattractive and lose their sexual viability. Only when they have a partner, usually a man, does their sexuality leap into life. Secondly, you may find yourself hanging on to a relationship in spite of a lot of hurt and problems to yourself, simply because you do not want to be left *alone,* because that will mean that your personal value has disappeared with your partner.

'**Sex is for the young and attractive and available.**' Let us look at each of these prerequisites in turn. Young – what does this mean? And what does attractive mean? Usually we resort (with massive endorsement from the media) to slim youthful lines, some kind of attractive norm defined by someone else with some commercial interest in mind. And available – does this mean marriageable? Of childbearing age? A figure that will cause a few stirs, provoke a few wolf-whistles, turn a few heads? Whatever it means, many of us fall foul of it. Many women consider themselves out of the running because they believe middle age means they are 'past it'.

'Sex is sanctionable only in marriage.' Notice the word *only*. Of course sex is fine within marriage. The difficulty occurs if you think only in those terms. Many single women, widows, divorced women are harassed by this myth. And maybe women prefer to relate to other women or to more than one partner at one time.

Assertiveness in Sexual Situations

So when we look at the subject of sex and assertiveness, we know it is explosive and that we need to go carefully but that does not alter the fact that we still need to go! The same themes apply in the bedroom as they do in the supermarket or office: difficulty with making clear and specific requests; saying 'no' clearly and firmly and directly to sexual activity when you do not want it; staying out of the compassion trap and not automatically conceding your needs and wants as less important than your partner's; the need to recognize your feelings of anger, hurt and fear and to express them assertively; the need to be familiar with your body and your responses; not allowing your fear of criticism and disapproval to dominate your behaviour in your relationship; how to make a constructive change or initiate a constructive dialogue in a relationship that has become stuck or unsatisfying.

When the list of difficult situations is completed at the beginning of a course, the sexual situations or those with intimate partners are most often found among the 9s and 10s. It is easy to understand why such situations should be among the most difficult. As you will by now have realized, truly assertive communication and behaviour is more likely when your anxiety is lowest. So given a combination of general stress about the topic, your own difficulty in separating myth from fact, the anxiety about communicating with people who are most important to you and with whom you feel most vulnerable, it is easy to see why assertiveness in sexual situations requires a chapter all to itself.

Let us look at the sort of situations that can occur in women's lives, which represent the need to learn assertive skills within a sexual context:

Betty, thirty-eight, widowed six years ago, is beginning to relate to a new male lover for the first time. She has two children, aged ten and twelve, and has maintained a low sexual profile since her husband's death. Now faced with her new lover she lacks confidence. She feels like a novice again – she knows what she wants but feels unable to talk, to find the actual words to ask him to do things differently. She can respond passively as she has up until now, letting the situation continue, with her resentment building up steadily. She can let this go on until she explodes about what a lousy lover he is; or what may happen is that, like Ivy, she will find some indirect means of saying 'no' to him, cutting him off. She will probably avoid sex by saying that the children are unhappy with him staying the night, using that as an excuse. Her assertive option is to say how she feels, ask for a specific change, using the process described in Chapter 12.

Heather, thirty-eight, has enjoyed her marriage for fifteen years, but feels that sex with her husband has become routine, predictable and dull. She wants to find ways of renewing and reviewing their marriage and exploring new possibilities with each other.

Sarah is gay, and takes the brave step of joining a group on women's sexuality. She feels uncomfortable that all the other women in the group are married or only relate to men. She is the only one who has sexual relationships with other women. She simmers for a while and then blows up, accuses them of being biased, blames them for their rigid and bigoted beliefs. Making an assertive step could be to state that she feels isolated and that she would like her own lifestyle to be validated as well. She could also admit she needs support from other women in the group, as they are all facing exploration and discovery together.

Janet's marriage finished four years ago. At thirty-two, after a series of temporary flings, she decides she wants to remain celibate for a while, to step back and look at herself before getting involved with someone else. When she meets a man who asks her out, she is unable to make her limits clear. She is afraid of being labelled frigid, weird or 'bent'. Her anxiety in this situation pushes her into anticipating every situation as a potential attack. She overreacts and leaves both herself and the other person embarrassed. She has to practise making a clear statement at the beginning of the friendship, setting limits so that they know where they stand.

Marianne has not really wanted sexual activity since the birth of her first child, a year ago. Her husband has been kind and understanding but nevertheless has wanted sex so she has 'given in', even though it has sometimes been painful for her. She is trapped in believing that it is her duty after all, she is his wife and if she does not give him what he wants, he may go and find it elsewhere. An assertive option is to talk about it to her husband and negotiate a compromise around what kind of sexual activity they both want: for instance, oral sex as an alternative to sexual intercourse. Another assertive option could be to seek outside counselling if they felt unable to sort out the problem on their own.

Meg, unmarried, forty-five, is recently interested in sexual relationships with several ongoing partners. Her close friends of long standing are rather shocked by her behaviour and consider it little short of unseemly, at her age! She is worried about how to keep them happy and allows their disappoval to feed her own uncertainty about whether or not she is doing the right thing. She can choose to keep her friends from intruding on her own pleasure and enjoyment and assert her right to choose her own sexual lifestyle, making a clear statement to that effect if necessary.

Before attempting to make any changes in your own life, it is worth considering some rights which apply specifically in a sexual context.

   1. I have a right to whatever information I want about sexuality. This does not sound too much to assimilate until you think about the general attitude towards sex education. If you think how you learned about sexual behaviour, you will probably find that, like many people, it was a haphazard process of misinformation and mistakes and learning through experience. Probably even now, there is a lot you do not know but are afraid to ask. Reading, talking, asking questions is important. Talking to other women too with a spirit of enquiry rather than competition is a good beginning. Many of us talk to our best friends about important and intimate things, but not sex. Yet once you overcome this reluctance you may find you can learn a lot and that sharing your own experiences can be very fruitful. Joining a women's sexuality group if there is one near you could be another way of finding out. It is important too to obtain factual information; this is why it is helpful to talk with friends you trust and who are not trying to impress you. Many magazine articles give some facts but others exhort you to be better and sexier for your partner. Beware of society's norms, which bring us to the second right:

   2. I have the right to choose my own sexuality. By this I mean the right to sort out for yourself the person you are and want to be sexually. This may mean not being sexually active at all; or relating to one man or to one woman, to several men at once or to several women; to both men and women at the same time; to be married and monogamous; to be single and monogamous; whatever anyone else thinks is right for you needs to be considered in the light of what you consider right for yourself at any given stage of your life. What suited you at twenty may not suit you at fifty.

3. I have the right to ask for what I want sexually. Many women balk at the idea of saying what they want because they risk appearing selfish. It also confuses the issue because you cannot ask for what you want until you know what it is. We will look at this further in the section on communication. Selfish it may be, but it is a useful antidote to the idea that there is nothing in it for you. If sex is only for the convenience of your partner, then you do yourself a great disservice and devalue yourself very deeply. This also confronts the belief that as a woman you are there only to respond to the man. Taking a more active role, asking and asserting your equal right to enjoyment is an important way of learning to take an equal part in bedtime activities. Traditionally, of course, this is the man's role but they too can often be persuaded to be relieved of this onerous responsibility – you may be surprised!

4. I have the right to sexual pleasure. The emphasis here is on the word pleasure. Enjoyment. Fun. Frolics. For this, of course, you need to feel friendly and relaxed towards the person you are with. If either of you is being too serious or heavy, then fun is usually out. Instead of making it all a chore, you can consciously decide to let go and enjoy yourself. This has a lot to do with your body, understanding how it works, how you respond and essentially trusting yourself enough to let go. We seem to carry round a little personal prude with us which sits on our shoulder and just when we are beginning to get that old smile on our faces and our toes are beginning to tingle, up it pops with a frown and a leer, reminding us sternly there are other things we should be attending to, that we should not let go, make too much noise, move about too much, show we are enjoying it too much, come too quickly, too loudly, too often, take too long and so on. An endless stream of killjoy messages, guaranteed to bring us down to earth just when we want to be taking off for the skies!

Giving yourself permission to receive enjoyment from someone else is very important. Believing you deserve time and attention and a little adoration here and there! Taking time for yourself ties in with being selfish. You do not have to regard your body as a vehicle for someone else's satisfaction only – there can be something in it for you if you want.

5. I have a right to choose my form of sexual enjoyment. Just as you have the right to choose who you want to enjoy yourself with, if anyone, then you have also a further right to decide *how* you want to have fun. Again, the experts, the gurus and the mass media tell us which positions, which type and how many orgasms are best, how long and where to do it, what to do before and after. Once you have spent some time finding out about your body, learning about your responses, becoming familiar with what turns you on a little, what blows your mind and what definitely turns you off, you will have a better idea of what conditions you need to enjoy yourself. Conditions may be warmth, time, safety, being cherished, privacy – things like that. Take the time to discover and find out about yourself.

6. I have the right to change my mind. There is a huge cultural pressure which makes it almost impossible for us to get started into something sexy and then realize that one's heart is not really in it, that what we would really prefer would be a cup of tea or a good sleep or a walk round the block, but can we say so? Can you acknowledge your right to change your mind? Rarely. And if you are feeling sexy at five o'clock when your lover telephones and find at seven o'clock that, several crises later, you are not at all in the same frame of mind; but in charges your lover, expecting you to be hot and panting, so what can you say? Nine times out of ten, you find yourself going along with it, feeling guilty because you are feeling different, because you are going to let someone down, be considered disappointing, or maybe even called a prick-tease. It does not help either that there seems to be an accepted line of progress towards intercourse. You may start with a kiss and enjoy it, and maybe you are happy with a cuddle, but the last thing you feel like is *that*! But what do you say? Can you assertively extricate yourself and say you really do not want to make love? Can you assertively set your limits in this way? And do you know what your limits are in the first place?

Sex and the compassion trap. Most women I have met admit that they have participated in some kind of sexual activity without really wanting to at one time or another. They have done so feeling reluctant, half-hearted, sometimes in physical pain, yet have still agreed to have sex and not made a clear refusal.

If you ask yourself whether you too have said 'yes' to some kind of sexual activity when in truth you really wanted to say 'no', then see if any of the following reasons are similar to your own:

Fear of being accused of being frigid or a tease.

Fear of it meaning that you *are* frigid, that there is something wrong with you.

Fear of a hostile response, of being attacked verbally or physically.

Fear of provoking an argument and then having a grumpy partner who turns over in a huff and fidgets through the night so you do not get any sleep.

Fear of rejection if you do not say 'yes' and then feeling lonely.

To prevent your partner from looking elsewhere for satisfaction.

Assuming it is your duty – because you are his wife, or because you have been treated to an evening out. Or was he a comfort to you when you needed it?

Do not assume that only women fall into this sexual compassion trap. Men also fall into the same trap: making love with someone when they are not in the mood. Mechanical sex of any kind usually hides other feelings. Not wishing to hurt the other person's feelings, be rejecting, appear ungrateful, not wanting to lose them to someone else . . . the trap is the same: forever assuming that the other person's needs are more important than your own.

One of the great signposts that you are about to fall into the trap is when you catch yourself thinking, 'Well, I'll probably warm up a bit . . . given a little time, I'll probably get in the mood.' This can and does occur and, with luck, your own enjoyment will neutralize any feelings of doing it for the other person. Very often, however, that warm-up does not get warm enough, it does not quite take off and you do not ever really feel as engaged as you could do.

Again in both heterosexual and homosexual relationships many of us assume one of two roles. The first is a parental role – this may emerge as a loving maternal sense or a wifely sense of obligation but either way there is no equality of right or choice. Saving someone from being disappointed or rejected fails to take into account your own fear of disapproval and criticism. The second role is more child-like, stemming more from a desire to please and to be appreciated, to belong and be accepted. Sometimes we avoid saying 'no' as adults because we do not want to risk losing out on this all-important affection and approval.

Saying 'no' and keeping to it is compounded it seems by the 'passive nature' of the vagina. When a man wants to say 'no' then there simply is no erection. When a woman wants to say 'no' but fails to assertively, then it is relatively easy for her to assume a passive position (literally) and to allow a man inside without resistance. Even though there is no apparent resistance, and many women will stoutly deny their feelings by saying 'I don't really mind', there is often an indirect reaction. Sometimes the vagina and the rest of the genital area become completely numb so that the woman cannot feel anything at all; sometimes the vaginal muscle goes into a tight spasm and her body says 'no' for her. Gradually she may cut herself off from all her sensations so that after months, years, she ends up feeling nothing at all – her whole body says 'no'.

Myth versus fact. This underlines the importance of information. Many women act on false assumptions not only about female sexuality but about male sexuality as well. Two particular myths are helpful to understand when trying to stay out of the sexual compassion trap.

Man is a sexual beast: he has uncontrollable needs. Once he is aroused and has an erection, he has to find some relief, otherwise he will explode or implode – one way or another it will do him untold harm. Although there is no evidence to support this, many men and women continue to believe this and women feel very guilty and can be made to feel guilty enough to 'do something' about an erection. Another common belief is that as you have 'caused' the erection, it is your responsibility to do something about it yourself, and give him some relief. You can see evidence of this belief in the extreme example of women being accused of being responsible for their own rape.

The question of arousal and erection is not as straightforward as it appears. A man cannot control whether or not he has an erection. The mistaken belief that a man can 'move it up and down' at will can cause a woman to feel rejected if her partner fails to get an erection when she wants one and to be offended if he gets one when she does not want it.

The man must initiate and perform: this leads women to avoid refusals because they do not want their male partner to feel inadequate. They do not want to take the initiative themselves because they think the man should know what to do. They shirk from asserting their own needs clearly and specifically because the man should be in charge and anyway, if he loved you enough . . .

Women still have a long way to go in taking responsibility for their own pleasure in sexual situations. Taking an active and equal part in a relationship with a partner allows you to say 'no' (and 'yes') assertively, to get your needs met and to be yourself in bed instead of achieving some mythical goal or standard.

Reviewing your sexual attitudes and wants and priorities can take time – it certainly requires interest and motivation. For the time being, we can look at how assertive skills can be applied to this area of our lives and put into practice in sexual situations. Consider Agnes, Dulcie, Ivy and Selma in action:

Example 1. You have been out to dinner on your first meeting with a man, then back to your place for coffee. You come face to face with the classic assumption that coffee is merely a euphemism for sex. It is getting late and he is getting amorous. This leads to a caress which leads to a grope which leads to him getting noticeably aroused. You are tired and want to go to bed . . . alone.

Agnes's tactics: she turns round and yells, 'leave me alone. Who do you think I am?' Or with a little touch of Ivy she goes along passively but inside thinks 'okay buster, let's see what you're made of, let's see how you perform'. The likelihood is that the man will sense this aggression and lose the ability to 'perform' anyway.

Dulcie's tactics: she may attempt to push his hands away and mutter something like 'I really am very tired, it's getting late'. Her confusion and perhaps misplaced guilt keep her locked in passivity. So she allows herself to submit to sex right there on the settee.

Ivy might attempt an indirect repulse like 'I'd love to but it's the wrong time of the month'. Or 'I don't feel very well', (feeling, like Dulcie, afraid to be called a prick-tease or frigid and afraid to make him angry). She may win by making him feel guilty enough to go home. She may go ahead anyway but get her own back later, for example, by spreading defamatory rumours to mutual acquaintances: 'My dear, he was lousy, all talk and no action; he couldn't get it up to save his life.' These put-downs can temporarily relieve the feeling of unfairness and bitterness and anger at allowing oneself to be used yet again. Remember the 'no' will always come out somehow!

How would Selma deal with it? She could say 'no', for a start, which is a word missing from many women's attempts to refuse. Keeping out of the Compassion Trap, the conversation might go like this:

Selma: Look, it's late, I would like to go to bed alone.
Man: But you're so attractive you are really turning me on. *(Manipulative bait.)*
Selma: I am attractive, yes, but I don't want sex with you right now, I want to go to bed alone.
Man: But it would just round off the evening nicely.

Selma: It would for you, but no, I don't want sex with you and I think it is time for you to leave.

Man: What are you, bent or something? *(Argumentative bait.)* Are you frigid or into women?

Selma: There's no point in being nasty. No, I don't want to have sex with you.

You can try:

'Yes, it has been a nice evening, but no, *I don't want sex with you tonight.*'

'No, I am not a prick-tease, *I don't want sex with you tonight.*'

'I can see that you are aroused but you could always masturbate: *I don't want sex with you tonight.*'

'I can see that you are angry, but *I don't want sex with you tonight.*'

'No, it is not something you did wrong. It is just *I don't want sex with you tonight.*'

Of course, it may be unlikely that you would find a person who persisted *so* strongly! But we are so often indirect that the message has a chance of slipping away unheard.

Example 2. In a situation which has escalated in a long-term relationship the problems are more acute. Let us take the example of a woman in a long-term heterosexual relationship where sex has been generally okay, but she just doesn't feel like intercourse. She is worried, tense, feeling overburdened and consequently distracted from pleasure.

Agnes's tactics: she might shrug aggressively as soon as her husband touches her and say 'Stop pawing me' or may start a row, knowing that sufficient distance would stave off enthusiasm and physical contact.

Dulcie may go along impassively or resort to indirect means like going to bed early or pretending to be asleep when he comes to bed or leaving in a tampon after her period has finished because she knows that this will make him leave her alone.

Ivy might opt for a 'headache' or a combination of the above-mentioned tactics. Afterwards, just as he makes the first move, she will bring up the subject of his mother knowing that his interest will soon be deflected; or she winces as he touches her so he will know something is wrong, feel guilty and draw back.

Selma can make a statement of how she is feeling – tired, unenthusiastic, lukewarm or whatever it is. She might suggest ways of changing the household arrangements so that she could have some help so as not to be so tired; or suggest that they make time to sort out together what was happening to their sex life; or make an assertive compromise like wanting to be close and affectionate but not sexual; wanting to stimulate orally or manually but not have intercourse. Whatever the option, she and her partner negotiate as equals, not out of compassion.

Assertive compromise or prostitution? Women feel very strongly about prostitution – some fight to honour it as a profession. Others claim it demeans female sexuality. Whichever way your own values fall, it is still an unavoidable image of female sexuality in our culture. It is worth raising the point here because even without an open financial transaction, many women sell their bodies for something other than cash. When you reach an assertive compromise with a partner, it is not the same as using your sex to bargain for the bathroom to be redecorated at the weekend or distracting him from getting angry with you, or keeping him hooked and happy. None of this is right or wrong, but it is important to be clear whether or not you are selling something in return for sexual favours granted. If you are not clear, then you will not be able to communicate assertively – you will have too much investment in what happens to follow the guidelines of constructive criticism.

Sex is certainly powerful and people disagree as to why it is so. Because many women have come to accept that they have what men want, they often use it dishonestly, aggressively, manipulatively. Sometimes women feel that this is the only real power they possess. I believe that reclaiming your sexuality for yourself is different from using the power you have to wield between your legs. Being angry and saying so directly can be a start in being able to claim equal sexual rights.

One of the first steps in looking at sexual relationships honestly is to watch for other feelings. This applies in both heterosexual and gay relationships. You will remember the chapter on feelings and how our feelings are related to different needs. We discussed that if the feelings are not expressed directly, they will come out sideways. One of the times they emerge is in a sexual context – because when we are intimate and close, we are ourselves more vulnerable.

It can be useful to look at how other feelings – that is, apart from purely physical sexual feelings – can get in the way of enjoyment and pleasure. Unexpressed anger for example can come out in a refusal and withdrawal from sex – either aggressive or indirect.

Anxiety about doing the right thing or about being loved and valued and approved of can interfere with your level of sexual arousal. The need for closeness or to share some sadness can interfere with the ability to feel pleasure of a sexual kind. Sometimes we get into a sexual situation, not because we feel particularly horny but because we want a cuddle and affection and rather than leave it at that, we are then forced or force someone else into something further. When unexpressed feelings lie festooned around the bedroom, they usually interfere and contaminate. Hostility breeds fear which breeds alienation and silence – sex becomes an empty, mechanical echo, loveless, and dishonouring, with the two people in some bizarre paradox of intimate physical contact, in their hearts isolated, afraid and alone.

So how to avoid all this? How to make sex friendly, warm, erotic and fun? Let's examine assertive communication as a final part of this chapter. What best describes your own way of communicating: accommodation or negotiation?

The first thing to note is that you start off from an equal position.

Shared responsibility. Accommodation is the passive option – you may think you are being equal but you are really fitting in with the other person's needs, anything for a quiet life and so on. You may adopt a sort of maternal role, feel sorry for them, forgive their shortcomings, rather like those of a child. Or you may prefer to hold on to the idea that your partner is perfect and not want to acknowledge their shortcomings as if the idea of imperfection makes you too insecure.

Blaming is the aggressive option – tempting but disastrous in terms of clear communication as we have already discussed. It is easier to allow someone else to bear the brunt of your own non-assertive behaviour and its consequences. Before you launch into blaming, remember it takes two: even if you have suffered someone's bumbling fingers groping over your body for twenty years and you feel like exploding with self-righteous venom and fury! Blaming encourages us to use such epithets as 'You're such a lousy lover' or 'You're as responsive as a choc ice', 'There must be something wrong with you, you're abnormal'. Remember to preface your statements with how you feel, and this should be easier now you've practised: 'I feel', 'I would like', 'I find it difficult', 'I'm afraid', 'I don't know when you're aroused', 'I'm unwilling to let go'.

Negotiation is equal – you are in it together and you want to make it work. This may not always be the case, but if it is, proceed as follows.

Talking is important. The difficulty is that we have usually learned early on that to talk about sex is to lose the magic, to break the spell, that it should just be natural and you should not really have to speak about it. This creates three difficulties: one, you feel guilty and foolish and as if you are being a real killjoy if you bring it up, that you are dull and putting an unnecessary dampener on the proceedings and making it too serious. Secondly, we are hampered by believing that 'Mr Right' exists – and that if your lover were sensitive and really loved you and were utterly attuned to you, then they would know what to do, how to send you into ecstasy, would touch the right places. And saying there is something wrong feels like a put-down, that it is *their* fault. They are going to feel offended, inadequate and in the wrong – precisely because, somewhere, you think they *are* in the wrong! Thirdly, we are so stuck in the silence that we have forgotten the vocabulary: we do not know what words to use. They feel awkward and clumsy or clinical and distant. With practice you can overcome this problem. Two helpful guidelines are: choose your moment and request a change.

The moment is not in bed! If you wait to criticize your lover in bed, no matter how assertively you are inclined, you risk provoking a defensive response. A male lover may well lose his erection and blame it on you. But, even so, the atmosphere is usually so highly charged that you are better advised to talk at a completely separate time of the day, neither just before sex or during or after.

Keep it brief and clear. You do not have to have a seminar about it – resorting to non-verbal communication can be enough but is sometimes misleading – some groans and grunts sound the same whether they are saying 'more, more' or 'that's enough'.

Remember the museum again (see Chapter 12), particularly if you are confronting a situation in an established relationship. Deal with one thing at a time and remember it's a joint venture. Be direct and specific about what you do want – help your lover to know how to be more loving, to give you more attention and so on.

The purpose of assertive criticism is to be constructive. It means looking at the positive strengths of your relationship as well as the weaknesses. It means being open to receiving criticism yourself and being prepared to accept some of the responsibility for change. This is quite different from launching into a blistering attack on the other person's performance or using your criticism as a weapon of subtle vindictiveness. Finding out, taking responsibility for yourself, giving yourself information are all ways of adopting an assertive approach to your own sexuality. There are many ways of doing this if you want to and some helpful books for further reading are listed at the back of this book.

I would like to finish with a story I heard which, for me, provides an inspiring example of one woman's assertive approach to her own sexuality. The woman in question was seventy-four – she had very recently met a man in a shop while buying curtains. They fell in love and after a few months, which is when I was told the story, she decided to have plastic surgery on her hip/pelvis, because she wanted to be more active and to have more sexual pleasure with her new lover!

Following on

1. Take some time to read about women's sexuality and find out for yourself – see Further Reading page.

2. Talk to someone close about your feelings about sex. Honest sharing can be another important way of learning.

3. If you have difficulty finding the words to use when you want to communicate, take ten minutes to write down on a piece of paper *all* the words you know for genitals, activities – slang words, clinical words – just to help yourself feel less anxious about them. You could even go one step further and say them aloud in front of a mirror.

4. Learn what turns you on, what you find erotic, and pleasurable. The books mentioned can give you ideas how to do this.

5. Identify three things which you could do and three things which your partner(s) could do to make sex more pleasurable. The next step is to communicate these assertively using the guidelines described in this chapter.

16

A Personal Enquiry

Up until this chapter, we have looked in detail at what happens during the process of communication with others. We have been looking at how you put yourself across and how to do so more effectively and clearly and honestly. If you try out any of the relevant assertive skills, whether in role-play or in reality, you will probably become more aware of your self-image and the image that it is important for you to present to other people. Until we try and change, we are often not so conscious of the impressions we are striving to make, simply because we usually behave out of habit. Change of any kind brings excitement and new challenges. It can also make us temporarily confused as unexpected conflicts come into view.

Even if you decide to act assertively and succeed, you may worry about the effect your behaviour is having on other people. Near the end of an assertiveness class, Viv came back from holiday with the following story: On the flight out, she had sat by choice in a non-smoking area. When a man in front of her had lit up a cigar, she wrestled with herself for a moment then mustering all her assertive determination, she leant forward and quietly asked him to put it out. He was a little taken aback, but nothing serious. And he did as she asked. All well and good, you might think, the end of the story. But then, Viv went on, her agony started. The passenger's wife turned round and gave Viv a long, penetrating look. What was actually in that look we will never know, but what Viv saw was the sort of shock and disapproval she might have expected had she lifted up her skirt and exposed herself. This triggered off a spiral of anxiety and uneasiness in Viv. She sat there pretending to read, her stomach knotted, wondering what on earth they thought of her! No matter how much she told herself rationally that they did not matter, that they were strangers she was never going to see again, that she had been quite within her rights to ask, the torment continued for about twenty minutes! Even at the airport at the other end, she noticed she was avoiding them. How silly, you may think. In some ways, yes, but very understandable. Even sillier perhaps to pretend that behaving assertively will not bring you face to face with surprising elements of yourself: who you are, what you want, and how you feel and what you hide from others. Part of the confusion in getting to know yourself stems from a dependence on *reflections*.

A woman looks in mirrors everywhere to see how she appears to others. She also looks to others, to the mirrors in people's eyes, to tell her how she appears. In the mirror she sees one image. In someone's eyes, she sees another. Maybe in someone else's eyes she sees yet another. The images may conflict or converge. Sometimes she thinks that the reflections show all of herself; not a part of her, but all there is of her. So the reflections become important. They reassure, they are evidence of her existence. What is more, they give her credibility.

When the eyes smile, she assumes approval; she assumes she has done well, what was expected of her. She has earned approval and acceptance in their eyes. If she makes a positive statement about herself, she will look to the eyes for endorsement. She becomes accustomed to relying on reflected judgement.

We develop 'winning ways'; we become expert at responding to other people's cues, testing the ground for approval, making the right impression, matching and adapting our actions, words and movements. If we look to these eyes for judgement and approval, the extent will be clearly marked if and when we consider a change in our behaviour. 'But what will they think of me?' becomes a frequent refrain. Obviously, if we choose to live, work, sleep, talk, travel, and share our lives with other human beings, it would be useless to stay in a vacuum or to close our eyes and ears to everyone else. The trouble is that many women are *so* dependent on outside approval and confirmation that instead of a balance between their perceptions and others' perceptions they become too caught up with the external impression. Listening to the chatter of the judgement outside, they stop listening to their own voices within.

Self-Esteem

It follows on from here that if we are too caught up with the reflections in the mirror, then we will look there to find not only a confirmation of self but also a confirmation of worth.

Self-esteem is wrongly confused with conceit and arrogance. It is wrongly assumed to be dependent on success. Self-esteem stems from a strong, rooted sense of self-worth which survives both failure and success; it survives mistakes, disappointment, and most of all self-esteem survives acceptance and rejection from others.

You certainly know when you are low on self-esteem. There is no mail for you, a friend forgets you never take milk in your coffee, a stranger scowls at you – and your feeling of worth plummets to the ground. You are left wondering what you have done wrong. What have you done to deserve this? But, on good days everything you do feels right. You can dismiss a frown, a disapproving comment, because you feel strong enough in yourself.

Two of the major ingredients of self-esteem are the feelings of being accepted and being loved.

Acceptability. It is natural to want to be accepted. It is natural to want to belong, to fit in with those who are important to us. If this part of your self-esteem, if how acceptable you are depends on how others see you and rate you, then it will be more difficult to take the risk of trying something different, which might not be as acceptable to those on the outside. To get an idea of how this might apply to you, take a look at the different roles you have in your life and see if you can identify the spoken and unspoken expectations of those roles. It often happens that what we do by choice can also fit in with others' expectations. Sometimes, though, we find ourselves in conflict with a given condition of acceptability.

We can be over-influenced by the power of the reflected image which damages our self-esteem. A single woman in her fifties may not feel acceptance when she looks in the mirror. She feels her right to feel acceptable as a woman depends on her being young, attractive and attached. Since she sees in herself none of these 'qualifications', she does not look for it in other people's eyes. She does not receive reflected approval and she rejects herself.

You can step out of line and make a bold move for yourself and still be haunted by uncertainty. Another woman looks in the mirror. She has started a job to make a life of her own, which has meant someone else caring for her family some of the time. She discovers how much she relied on reflected approval since she does not get it any longer from her particular circle of people. She sees sometimes real and sometimes imagined disapproval in their eyes. She wonders if being a woman really does mean being a selfless and devoted mother. She looks at herself and experiences the discomfort of not knowing who she is any more. Before she can discover herself in her own right, there will be a period of anxiety and conflict. We can assess how much of our behaviour is based on a need for reflected approval and how much is a choice we make for ourselves. Somewhere there is a balance. What do you see when you look in your mirror?

Whose eyes reflect back your measure of acceptability? What standards do you have to measure up to? Whose standards need you reach in order to qualify for acceptance within each category of your life? Do you have to be happily married? Have an attractive figure? Be a perfect mother? A sparkling hostess? A sexually satisfying partner? A socially-conscious citizen? A charitable neighbour? A grateful daughter? A competent housewife? An active feminist? A dependable friend? An inspiring leader? An inventive cook? A reliable worker? An uncomplaining saint? A tower of strength for others?

Once you can see how much you depend on others for a feeling of acceptance, you can also see the possibilities for building a sense of *self*-acceptance. This need not exclude others completely but can help to shift the balance a little so you have more room to manoeuvre. You can give yourself more permission to express yourself in the ways that you choose.

Desirability. This goes hand in hand with acceptability to make a powerful combination. Being loved gives us a feeling of confidence which is almost unbeatable. But feeling unloved and undesirable makes us feel miserable, wretched, useless. It regenerates itself so that if we feel loved, we feel lovable. This makes us attractive and people love us more, so we continue feeling lovable . . . and it works in reverse as well. The loss of love for short or long periods of time can run dangerously into the feeling of being unlovable; this makes us desperate and clinging which in turn makes us unlovable so we continue to feel unloved and undesired.

We all fear rejection. And we all experience it. However much we may try and prevent it happening, rejections both slight and serious occur throughout our lives. The following examples give an idea of the sort of situations you might experience as rejecting. See if you can identify with any of them.

1. Someone forgets your birthday or an important anniversary.

2. You are feeling very enthusiastic about something that has happened to you but your partner couldn't care less.

3. You reach out to give someone some physical affection and they withdraw.

4. One of your parents continually compares you unfavourably with others.

5. Your partner criticizes your appearance.

6. You offer to do someone a favour and you are turned down.

7. You are turned down after an interview.

8. Someone you are attracted to tells you 'I don't want to be your lover'.

9. You show something you have written or something you have made to someone important in your life and they criticize it heavily.

10. You give someone a present you have chosen carefully and they are unimpressed.

11. You don't get an invitation to a meeting or party to which everyone else seems to have been invited.

12. You feel like making love but your partner isn't in the mood.

Our experience of rejection will be affected by the importance of the particular person rejecting us, our own individual 'crumple buttons' (see Chapter 11) and our mood at the time. Sometimes it takes a lot to shift our self-esteem; and at other times, just a single glance or a tiny gesture is enough to trigger off a whole rush of past unresolved and unexpressed feelings of rejection. Given that we are bound to experience rejection in some form or other throughout our lives, it is useful to know how to handle it assertively.

There are two ways: long-term and short-term.

The long-term strategy is to learn the skill of loving yourself, something which we often find difficult. Learning how to be a friend to yourself day-by-day will stand you in good stead in an emergency. If you have built up a reserve of self-sustenance on the inside, you can withstand many pressures and assaults from the outside. Like laying in stores for a rainy day.

Exploring the positive aspects of solitude. Do you enjoy your own company? How do you approach periods of solitude? Do you look forward to them as a welcome relief? Do you dread them? Do you spend your time doing whatever you enjoy doing – even if that happens to be nothing at all – or do you spend the time fretting and worrying about everyone else? Being on your own is also a good way of finding out what is actually happening on the *inside*, especially important when so much of our lives is taken up with concern for what is happening *outside*. Just a few minutes each day, a few hours each week can be enough to remind yourself that there is a part of you to be noticed, to be attended to, listened to and cherished.

Learning about your relationship with yourself and the way in which you react with everyone and everything around you can help you rely more on yourself and less on external confirmation.

Short-term strategies for coping with rejection involve keeping afloat in the shallows rather than disappearing into the deep end. We have discussed ways of coping with rejection in a class through women sharing their own methods of being good to themselves in a crisis. They have looked at how to hold on to the feeling that they are worth being loved, that they are still *lovable*, even though they may not feel loved at that moment. Here are some examples of their antidotes to rejection:

A walk by the sea/in the country.
A gin and tonic.
Music.
Phoning a good friend who loves you.
Being with people who love you.
Sleep.
Writing out your feelings.
Having a good cry.
A treat of some kind.

Linking Self-image, Self-esteem and Assertiveness

How does Dulcie see herself? Dulcie escapes into daydreams, where she sees herself as ideal – the queen, the boss, the star – to avoid looking at herself in reality. She sees herself as hopeless, helpless and inadequate. She identifies with this image so much that she convinces others of the truth of it. Her self-esteem is very low. She looks to others to give her a sense of purpose and identity. If she is accepted by others, then she feels loved, but only a little – it is never enough.

And Agnes? She punishes the vulnerable and fragile parts of herself that allow her to feel hurt. She keeps them firmly locked away. She is quick to get in first before she is attacked, rejects before she is rejected. Her self-esteem looks high but isn't and she is often quite desperate to be loved and accepted even though she would rather die than admit it.

Ivy appears to think highly of herself. She seems to be quite satisfied and confident. But secretly, she subjects herself to all sorts of critical pressures and punishes herself pitilessly when she fails to meet her own expectations. In order to avoid rejection, she holds on more and more tightly to the control in her relationships, ever more desperate to earn approval.

Selma expresses herself in the real world, not only in her imagination. She accepts herself as she *is,* which means acknowledging her strengths and weaknesses. The more she values herself and feels strong in herself, the more she can allow herself to look at those parts of herself which she does not like very much but can accept. The more she accepts herself with her limitations, the more she is open to listening to other people's criticism and learning from it, without sinking into self-reproach. The more open she feels, the more she is free to be herself. She can take the risk of changing without clinging desperately to the known and familiar.

She conveys her certainty of her own value as well. She is open to acceptance and love from others: if she experiences rejection, she is not demolished: her self-esteem is anchored within herself and this helps her to survive hurt and disappointment. If she is not accepted by others she can choose to weigh up the importance of their approval against the importance of doing what she wants to do for herself.

From a base of self-esteem, she is able to take the risk of changing. With a basic belief in herself, she can go on to find further ways of self-expression. From a base of certainty in herself, she can risk the uncertainty of change.

Following on

1. Write down a list of situations you find rejecting. Then consider what exactly you felt at the time: ignored? unheard? unimportant? hurt? resentful? invisible? not good enough? Next, note down what you actually said at the time. Did you express those feelings or not? If not, why not? Finally, think how you would like to have handled

the situation assertively or how you would handle a similar situation in the future?

2. Since self-esteem is so much tied up with our need for approval, it is interesting to explore this in more detail. Consider whether there is a person in your life whom you are aware of wanting to please. You cannot be yourself, you worry constantly about what they might think, you feel inhibited and uncomfortable in their company and worry that they do not or will not like you. With this in mind, answer the following questions, perhaps go through it aloud with a friend.

a) What does this person not like about you?

b) Is this based on impression or evidence? What sort of evidence?

c) What difference would it make if this person were to like you?

d) What do you need to do to get this person to like you? Are you honestly prepared to do it?

The answers to these questions will tell you whether your worry is absurd or whether you are genuinely worried about the person's opinion. If this is so, you can practise applying the skills of negative assertion and negative enquiry (see Chapter 11).

3. Imagine yourself as a very dear friend – a friend to whom you would like to express affection and appreciation. What small token of esteem can you give yourself? A bunch of flowers? A weekend being looked after in a hotel? A sauna? Special soap? A walk in the park? An early night? Find some way in which to treat yourself every single day.

17

The Power at the Centre

Another important ingredient of self-esteem is power. Some women react to being called powerful with alarm – assuming that being powerful means being domineering or threatening. We confuse power with oppression, having power *over* someone else. The assertive meaning of power is not the power of intimidation but power that comes through finding and being yourself. It is often the most difficult of all aspects of their behaviour for women to manage assertively – passively, we give away power, aggressively we use it to denounce and punish others, and indirectly we use it manipulatively to get what we want and to maintain control.

Being assertively powerful starts with being yourself. As we saw in the last chapter, this is not as easy as it sounds, given our personal, cultural and social constraints. Finding your self and then being yourself is a tremendous challenge. But this is when you feel powerful – everything clicks into place and you feel strong.

The experience of using the simple technique of repetition, explained in Chapter 4, has enabled many women to understand this feeling of personal power which replaces the more familiar state of anxiety. Anxiety is our biggest enemy. It holds us back, makes us doubt our worth and ability, makes us worry about losing approval. As they continue to repeat the statement, women feel the shift of feeling from uncertainty, hesitation and doubt to conviction, determination and strength of purpose. Your mind, heart and body work in unison – that is the moment of being personally powerful. You are being yourself. Being spontaneous is powerful. Instead of inhibiting your impulsiveness by stopping to calculate whether or not you are likely to lose approval with a particular word or action, you can act spontaneously. This does not mean launching out inappropriately in all directions. It means taking the risk of blurting something out without censoring first, reaching out to someone in affection, following through on a suspicion or hunch, having fun, saying what you feel!

With practice the powerful experience of spontaneity can withstand the looks of astonishment as you leap to your feet to defend a dearly-held principle, or the disapproval as you temporarily shelve your adult mode of being for a quick swing in the children's playground. You can rise above the consternation as you inform your family tribe that you are going away for Christmas this year instead of entertaining all twenty-nine of them at home. You can cope with the dismay around you when you sweetly and firmly decline the annual 'honour' of sewing all costumes for the end-of-term play; you can handle the disapproving remarks of your family or friends as you change your style of hair or dress to suit yourself for once. You can even survive the embarrassment of discovering you have made a mistake or the twinge of rejection if your gesture or suggestion is met with a brush-off.

The experience of assertive power involves an inner shift of emphasis. When women first look at their own behaviour, they will often conclude that their own individual response will depend on who the other person is, whether they are old or young, male or female, hostile or friendly, and so on. This limits our feeling of competence because our frame of reference is completely dependent on the *other* person. Once you have the knowledge of yourself and know how you feel, you can be more confident and flexible from your centre. The certainty comes from *within* you, rather than waiting for someone else to make the first move and then reacting accordingly.

In *The Assertive Woman*, Phelps and Austin suggest the principle of action rather than reaction. It means making the first move. This could be initiating a conversation, a meeting, a confrontation. This way round, you can feel much more powerful than if you just sit around and wait for the inevitable to happen. This is particularly effective when you are faced with a situation which causes you some anxiety. You sit and fret, biting your nails, waiting for the phone to ring, the summons to be made, the axe to drop or the pain to go away of its own accord. An alternative is for you to get up and make the first move.

This was illustrated by the experience of a class participant. Geraldine was worried about a situation at work. She had had a bad experience working with a particular colleague two years previously and had heard on the office grapevine that he was to be transferred back to her department. This meant that they would have to work together again. When she role-played the situation in class, she first presented the situation as if her boss had called her in to tell her the news. She handled it reasonably well, but not as well as she wanted. I then suggested that she role-played it a different way. This time *she* took the initiative and instead of waiting to be called in, she anticipated the move and asked to see her boss in advance. This way she could express her concern and state her feelings very clearly *before* the event. She felt more powerful and consequently she handled the interaction much better.

Women's behaviour is often characterized by a pattern of waiting: waiting to grow up, to be asked to dance, for a proposal of marriage, waiting for a child to be born, to grow up, to leave school and leave home; always waiting, waiting for something to happen first.

Instead of waiting for something to happen, you too can take that first step. Maybe there are all sorts of things you have in mind to do: places you would like to visit, people you would like to get to know, a room you would like to paint, a subject you would like to know more about, something you would like to buy. If there is, just ask yourself what you are waiting for and see if any of the following reasons are among your own. Have you ever put forward any of the reasons below as an excuse for not making that first step? Tick the ones that are familiar:

What are you waiting for?

For someone to say they're sorry.
For the children to leave home.
For someone to hold your hand.
For someone to show you the way.
For someone to give you their blessing.
For someone to say they're wrong.
For the sun to shine.
For your premium bond number to come up.
For someone to do it for you.
For someone else to make the first move.
For someone to give you a good kick.
For someone to make it safe for you to jump.

For someone else to say they'll be there in the end.
For someone to come back to you.
For someone to die.
For someone to forgive you.
For someone to mend the stepladder.
For someone to offer.
For someone to notice you.
For someone to sweep you off your feet.
For a knight in shining armour.
For the world to come to its senses.
For a diploma.
For someone to change her/his mind.
For someone to give you the go-ahead.

Being assertively powerful means doing something for yourself. A woman is often ready to put herself at the service of others at a moment's notice, to give up precious time, to expend valuable energy for *others*. But when it comes to a proposition for herself, then the story is different. The time and energy which stretch to infinity to accommodate the needs of others suddenly snap back — there is never the time for herself.

In Chapter 8, we examined ways in which we can get stuck in the compassion trap, which lead us to over-assume responsibility for the welfare of others. This can give us an indirect power, the power of feeling indispensable. Have you ever caught yourself dismissing a suggestion of a move, or change or rest for yourself, with an immediate retort on the lines of 'But they could never manage without me'? If you ask yourself whether or not you could really do without *them,* you quickly see how this trap works. However much we may complain about sacrifice and duty and responsibility, we may well be enjoying some kind of hidden spin-off. For example, if, when we look in the mirror of our self-image (see Chapter 16), we see predominantly the image of the tower of strength, it will be in this aspect that we will find fulfilment. If the only image of ourselves we have is of giver and carer, then we will need to make sure there are people around whom we can give to and care for. We can hold on, without realizing what we are doing, to those who are dependent on us — they can be a parent, a child, a partner, a friend, clients or patients — anyone who needs us in order to survive, we think.

Sometimes, confronted with a situation where we want to assert our own needs, to say no, to set limits on our time and energy, we do not feel enough motivation. So there is an automatic response of someone being too sick, or too old, or too weak, or too stupid, or too lonely or too inadequate or too young – in some way unable to survive without us. Sometimes the power of being indispensable provides a convenient way of hiding ourselves.

One unfortunate side-effect is what little of ourselves is seeking expression comes through indirectly. A familiar indirect strategy is guilt. Secretly we blame others and make them feel guilty but still our frustration grows. Understandably, it is difficult to let others feel free when we do not feel free ourselves. If we have not experienced a sense of our true assertive power, our personal power and potential, it is very difficult to be generous to others, to be happy that others are being true to themselves when we do not feel we are being true to ourselves. Allowing someone to do something for you, allowing yourself to receive for once, saying even just a small 'yes' for yourself is assertively powerful.

Assertive power is a power of equality and being direct about that equality. A friend of mine once remarked that the trouble with women was that they always came in through the back door, backwards. Much of this book has been encouraging a 'front door' approach instead – whether asking, refusing, confronting or expressing *directly*. But it is still difficult for women to give up that indirect hold on others. 'Let him think it was his *idea*,' is a phrase that embodies the covert attitude which exists towards men: on the outside smiling, nodding 'Yes, dear,' but on the inside, treating men like little boys who have scarcely learned to wash behind their ears: allowing yourself to be treated as inferior on the outside when you are certain you are superior on the inside. Behind this subtle expression of patronizing contempt exists a very real fear that any other way won't work and a fear of male authority and physical power. Being assertively powerful can provide an alternative method to this subterfuge.

It also means acknowledging responsibility. This does not mean taking the blame. It means the ability to look at your life and the people around you and acknowledge your part in the way it all is. This works in two ways: if your life is not to your liking, then instead of blaming others, look at ways of possible and reasonable change. Instead of pleading helplessness, and seeing yourself as an unfortunate victim, make choices – these may be to leave things as they are or to do something radically different or to compromise. The second way is to acknowledge responsibility for the good things in your life that you see – for your achievements, your efforts, your abilities. Respect yourself for what and who you are right *now*.

Finally, assertive power means making choices. The choice is to be the person you are, as opposed to always being the person you need to be in order to gain approval. And approval is more sinister than we think. We may escape from one set of regulations only to succumb to yet another, new set of regulations. A woman may discard the traditional feminine image and all the approval-seeking behaviour that she feels are part of that image – then to her surprise she finds herself caught up in a new set of approval-seeking behaviour. This time the image is feminist and more modern, but once again she finds herself restricted from choosing her own life-style or assessing her own behaviour independently. She finds herself again limited by the need to conform, to belong, to be approved of.

Making choices for oneself can build our sense of self-esteem.

Self-esteem – which embraces self-acceptance, self-care and self-realization – is vital. Learning the value of being assertive can be a powerful beginning.

Following on

1. Take the initiative to discuss a problem in a relationship or with your family rather than waiting until the problem arises again.

2. Write or telephone someone you would like to get to know to suggest a meeting.

3. Put yourself forward for promotional training at work instead of waiting to be asked.

4. Arrange a convenient time with your superior for a work review and assessment. Using the skills of negative enquiry, ask for constructive criticism but also ask for positive comments about your work and progress.

5. This is a longer exercise but an excellent way of discovering your priorities.

    a) Write down everything you want to achieve in your life: places to visit, topics to learn, what you want to make/write/build, what you want to own, how you want to enjoy yourself, what you want from your relationships, your work, your health. Write down every single goal you can think of, however unlikely, however small. This will be list A.

b) Write down which of these goals you would like to achieve in the next five years. This will be list B.

c) Write down a third list: which of these goals you would want to reach during the next year.

d) You now have three lists, A, B, C. Take list A and select 10 goals. Put them in order of importance so that Number 1 is the most important and Number 10 the least important. The process of deciding which goals you want to include is difficult but this is a crucial part of the exercise.

e) Take list B and select the ten most important goals and put them in order.

f) Take list C and do the same. If you do not have ten items for lists B and C, still put them in order so that Number 1 is the most important.

When you have finished you will have three final lists. Probably, the same goals will appear in all lists. What do these goals tell you about yourself? Which area of your life do they relate to? Can you use these lists to plan for further action? What are you waiting for?

18
Assertiveness as a Way of Life

Although this book has been concerned with specific skills, the more often we experience the positive feelings that come when we use those skills, the more central they become to our lives. Instead of feeling assertive and confident on a particular occasion, we begin to feel assertive and more confident *in general*.

Some of the hallmarks of this sort of approach to life include being more open and relaxed – less tense and defensive. Instead of having to keep all those nasty little flaws hidden away, you can relax and present the positive parts of yourself. Instead of feeling guilty about weakness and inadequacy, you learn to be less critical of yourself. You can listen to others because of a basic belief in yourself. You can also be more open to valid criticism. You can explore too the possibility of change, rather than holding on desperately to the old and habitual ways when you would be better to move on.

Remember it does not have to be you *versus* others. With time and care, you can learn to strike a balance between your needs and those of others, between your feelings and others', between your priorities and theirs. If you can handle change gently in yourself, you can handle change gently with others. Change of any kind threatens us with exposure or disruption. We fear loss and hurt. Coping with these anxieties is an important aspect of learning to be more assertive.

These anxieties are often temporary. People who are close to us can soon relax and enjoy the difference. Maybe you do not nag as much because you have learned to ask directly: you have stopped playing the helpless victim and are happier, doing something for yourself. You may have relaxed your frantic attempts to be super-woman. You do not have to make people feel guilty to get what you want. You do not have to make them squirm and suffer if they upset you but can express your feelings and then let it go. Having learned to be more accepting of your own limitations, you can be less exacting in your demands of others.

However, it can happen that the disruption can be more permanent. There may be those who simply cannot accept the new you. Some people are uncomfortable with change and would prefer you to stay the way you were – maybe it suited them better, maybe you were predictable and safer that way. Maybe they want to hold you back because they do not want you to accomplish too much and leave them behind. This brings inevitable conflict and only you can decide what you want to do and what your priorities are.

One frequent hazard to watch for is the hit-and-run approach. After years of feeling oppressed and restricted, you find out what you have been missing all this time. You may feel angry: 'All those times, I did what *he* wanted, what *they* wanted,' become ready fuel for action. This distorts our thinking and behaviour so that assertion degenerates rapidly into aggression. We state what *we* want, what *we* are going to do and then go off and do it, feeling satisfied with our new 'assertive' approach. But if the other person does not have a chance to speak, there is no room for negotiation. So although disguised as assertive behaviour, the attitude is more 'Like it or lump it', far more reminiscent of Agnes than Selma.

This happens out of anxiety. You feel if you do not get in quickly, someone will take away your option yet *again*, so you make sure you get your needs in first! This often stems from an accumulation of anger and blame from past experiences of the results of unassertive behaviour. If you remember that fifty per cent of the responsibility is yours, you can be more sensitive to others while *still* affirming yourself, and, with practice and confidence, you can achieve a genuine compromise.

Sometimes women find that learning assertive skills has an immediate and dramatic effect on their lives. But what they learn about themselves can set in motion a process of self-discovery through which they can understand their real potential.

I would like to finish with the words of some women who describe their own experience of learning to be assertive:

'I find I am using assertiveness in ordinary situations in my life and the more I use it the more satisfied I feel. I don't get left with feelings of resentment because I am no longer doing what I don't want to.' *Eileen*

'I'm clearer about the very fact of my existence, of me as a person, who I am and what I want to be. I really like myself more and more and I am much happier about taking criticism. I have a long journey ahead but that's okay.' *Mairead*

'Being assertive to me means taking myself and my needs seriously, taking risks in my personal relationships in order to be more honest, feeling the insecurity about changing, and discovering that I can be powerful without aggression or violence.' *Fiona*

'Assertiveness means being in touch with my own needs, feelings and specifically my power as a woman. It also means being able to confront myself and others and not take anything for granted. In the process of acknowledging my own needs, I am encountering anxiety and guilt which I will have to deal with. I feel that the development, while it will bring pain, will unleash the creative power of myself.' *Terri*

'Assertiveness means finding out why I behave the way I do, why I want what I want and then deciding whether this behaviour is really necessary or really me.' *Ursula*

'Learning to be assertive has meant that I no longer need to have so many rules for myself. I can handle a situation just for what it's worth, fresh and untouched by the usual trips I get into. It adds energy and excitement to my life and takes away a lot of fear and apprehension.' *Anne*

'I have found myself recently walking away from a few friends who are forever moaning and groaning . . . and I used to be so "kind"!' *Kathy*

'I am being assertive when I experience a sense of myself and can hold onto it no matter what I'm feeling. I then respect the same reality in the other person.' *Nellie*

'Assertiveness means respect for myself, the possibility that other people will really listen to me and therefore respect *me*. Being more open about my feelings.' *Anita*

'Learning the meaning of the word assertive has been a painful realization, but a beginning. I'm becoming aware of how seldom I ask for what I want, or take space for my own pleasures. Also how much of my identity is tied up in roles – mother, daughter, friend, group leader. I am beginning to rebuild and re-discover myself. It's a whole new fascinating exploration and, happily, turning out to be gratifying and affirming, like going through a pile of precious, forgotten objects in an attic.' *Marika*

It all takes time. The choices and changes are yours. What you find in the end is yourself.

1

Five Years On

Every morning, a thud on the doormat at the bottom of my stairs announces the arrival of assertiveness-training correspondence. Some of the mail is in direct response to the offer of details of classes at the back of this book; often it's a response to a particular radio, television or magazine feature; many are letters from readers writing to say how much the book has helped them. The correspondence is mostly from the UK but also from many European countries and sometimes from as far away as Africa, Australia and South America. Although the daily total is small, over five years it adds up to quite a lot of mail.

In addition there are phone calls every day from people interested in attending a class, sometimes reaching thirty or forty a day in response to a particular reference in an article or programme.

In the five years since this book was first published, I have watched assertiveness training grow from a minority interest to a large-scale phenomenon. It is taught as a regular evening class in Adult Education Centres throughout the UK, in rural as well as urban areas; in personnel and management contexts; in therapy groups in hospitals. It is part of many sixth-form curricula and most local education, government and medical authorities include it as training for their employees. It is recommended by GPs and psychiatrists for their patients and taught to nurses, playground attendants, librarians, prisoners, managers, mothers-to-be, midwives, teachers, students, nuns and secretaries.

Assertiveness training has always appealed to a wide range of people but what has changed in these five years is the extent to which, as a subject, it has been adopted into the main stream of education and training. In other words, assertiveness training has come of age; it has become respectable and is most definitely on the agenda.

Why has assertiveness training become so popular? Basically because it works! Assertive techniques and skills really do improve communication with family, friends, colleagues, strangers; anyone in fact with whom we have to interact. Many people have read my book, written expressly as a self-help book, and have been able to use the exercises at the end of the chapters to apply the techniques to their personal situations. The many thousands who have actually attended a course learn that practising the skills in a role-play situation is illuminating and clarifying. Role-play is also an extraordinarily effective way of learning both what fouls up communication, for example, unexpressed hostility or irrelevant waffle and what makes it more effective: directness, relaxed breathing and keeping to one issue at a time.

When we find something that really works, we usually tell others and the word spreads. For much of the time we amble through life wishing things could be different so that when we do find something that is immediately comprehensible and practical and can be applied to our own lives, our reported benefits and enthusiasm will inevitably generate more interest.

Assertiveness training is essentially optimistic. It offers a way to change and there is nothing so personally empowering as being able to change a situation which we genuinely believed was absolutely hopeless. If the classes are taught with integrity, the participants will learn that this process of change is possible through their *own* ability. We learn to be less dependent on others for advice and more reliant on self-understanding and self-direction. This is essential, particularly for women, who are discouraged by social conditioning from autonomy of thought, word or deed and who, for this reason, often find it difficult to make decisions independently of the approval of others.

As women develop more familiarity with the skills, they learn how to be more reflective in situations instead of reacting only to the other person. Thinking and consequently acting with more clarity improves self-confidence at a deep and fundamental level. Instead of muddling along, feeling generally burdened with worries and concerns, they learn to decide on priorities and to sort out who and what really does matter in their lives.

A further aspect which makes the experience of assertiveness training a positive one is the necessity for co-operation with others. In a class, and also through reading my book, people realize they are not alone, that everyone has similar problems and this simple yet vital observation relieves the numbing isolation from which so many people suffer. If I were to select a typical response from the thousands of letters I have received, it would be something like this: 'You've put your finger on it. Something I've felt for years, that I've known inside but haven't been able to express. Now I see it written down, I feel so much stronger, because I know I was right!' This experience of confirmation is expressed in many different ways, sometimes eloquent, often very moving. This has been the most rewarding aspect of my work for the past ten years, knowing all the time that I wasn't promoting the idea of anything new; I was offering an affirmation of something already there but which needed encouragement to find a voice.

Inevitably, any positive force for change will attract a negative reaction. Because of the very effectiveness and increasing popularity of assertiveness training, there has also been an increase in opposition and scepticism towards it. The first category of objections can be generally described as political. One criticism is that it encourages women to focus too much on themselves as individuals and their personal experience of oppression, thereby ignoring the important socio-political dimensions of women's oppression. If women only learn to improve their personal relationships within the existing structures, how can fundamental change take place?

My own belief is that the vast majority of women do not even begin to have a sense of their own destiny. The lion's share of a woman's physical, emotional and spiritual energy can easily be absorbed in meeting the demands of being a wife and mother.

Even more important is the constant energy required to worry about meeting real or imaginary expectations. Making things and people tidy and happy, appearing attractive, being seen to be ever-loving, self-sacrificing, successful and yet always maintaining a low enough profile to keep the boat steady. This preoccupation with how one is failing on the inside to meet outside needs and requirements is a terrible drain on personal resources. We can become so addicted to this profound sense of inadequacy that we do not find the time, energy or self-confidence to look, really look, at what is happening in the world outside our narrow lives. We ignore our right to have opinions and overlook our own potential impact on that world. Once a woman can see how she oppresses herself internally, she can become more deeply aware of oppression externally, not only her own but, especially important, of the oppression of others, even those quite outside her personal experience.

Another source of uneasiness is the especial popularity of assertiveness training among women, fanning fears that it is a feminist 'tool'. The sight of women flocking into evening classes in this subject when other more traditional classes are hard pushed to reach the minimum numbers, makes the authorities wonder what it is all about. Availability of classes at many of these institutes doesn't necessarily indicate an acceptance of the subject as a valuable addition to the curriculum; a more persuasive factor is the economic prospect of thirty or so eager participants ready to fill each course.

When I wrote my book, it was women who made up the bulk of the classes. Five years later, this situation is virtually unchanged. There are more mixed classes available and some classes for men only, but the number of men interested enough to attend a class remains comparatively small. There are several reasons for this. When women have been conditioned to be passive, uncomplaining, indirect and dependent, it is they who will more readily understand the frustrations and limitations of this kind of outlook and behaviour and will be ready to explore new ideas. Being open to new learning means being genuinely open to understanding the difference between assertion and aggression.

Aggressive behaviour is competitive, overriding, always lacking in regard for the other. It means winning at someone else's expense. Assertion is based on equality not superiority, co-operation not competition, honest and appropriate expression of feelings instead of ruthless suppression of them. It is based on a concept of power which is rooted in self-acceptance as opposed to the sense of power which comes from being bigger, stronger or wealthier than the next person. This is the fundamental challenge of assertiveness. We are so used to a world in which competition and comparison dominate all our relationships that it is hard to understand assertiveness is not about winning.

Acknowledging an assertive alternative confronts men with their own conditioning – be master of everything, hide your weakness, show your strength, get on top first or you'll go under. A man's response to these expectations will vary: he may feel personally enabled by them and use them as a rationalization to maintain a competitive lifestyle; he may feel personally disabled by them, and because the demands are too exacting, he may spend much of his life feeling he has failed as a man; he may be disturbed – realizing that although he knows he is apparently the winner, he wins at a cost of something precious, namely his humanity. Assertiveness training highlights the disadvantages of stereotyped behavioural expectations for both women and men but in order to be interested in changing the status quo, men have to feel unhappy with it. Only then will they be motivated to change it.

I believe men are further discouraged from learning about assertiveness training because attending a class demands participation, not only observation from the sidelines. Although some women are also reluctant to join a class for this reason, this anxiety is particularly relevant for men. When you are conditioned to hide weakness, it is hard to be vulnerable in public. Role-play participation involves a risk: you have to acknowledge that you do not have it all together, that you make mistakes and that there are situations which make you feel anxious and unconfident. Everyone feels anxious to some degree about role-play but once they have been through it they remember the support and encouragement from other participants and also their own sense of achievement.

The second category of criticism of assertiveness training can be described as clinical. Objections are raised by those who believe that any activity involving personal, emotional or psychological issues should be regarded as therapy and therefore should not be considered as education. These objections rarely come from professional practitioners themselves, who are often only too pleased to recommend their patients to attend a class. Ominous mutterings are more frequently heard from those who, I suspect, use this argument to add substance to their own fears. The main thrust of the objection equates attending an assertiveness training class with opening Pandora's Box.

According to the legend, Pandora's curiosity got the better of her. She opened the box and as a result, all sorts of dreadful ills and evils burst forth on to humankind. The analogy implies that assertiveness training is highly dangerous because if unsuspecting individuals open their personal 'boxes' they risk unleashing untold harm on themselves and others, and that this sort of psychological probing is best left either not done at all or conducted under the auspices of a medical professional.

The most insidious aspect of the Pandora analogy is that it plays on people's ignorance and consequent fear about feelings and the nature of emotions. There *is* some truth in the argument, but everything depends on how you perceive what happens. During a course, you focus on YOU: your behaviour, your relationships, your past experiences, your present and future expectations. In the process you may well discover that you have some feelings about what happens and what has happened to you – maybe anger at things you didn't say long ago, or hurt at others' behaviour. You may feel angry perhaps with yourself for not speaking up or being truthful or at 'wasted time'; you may uncover feelings of fear and rejection.

Feelings are an inevitable part of why we think and behave in the way we do. Part of the reason for a ten-week course is to allow time for some of these things to surface and be shared and to fall into place. In the teaching model I use and in which I have trained others, one complete session is devoted to the nature of feelings and another to the particular emotion of anger so that class members are able to see their feelings in perspective. For some, a little insight and self-confirmation is enough. For others, the class proves to be a beginning; maybe they will go on to pursue some of the past situations in individual counselling, learn further skills about managing feelings or seek out another class or area of study which seems appropriate at the time.

From my own extensive experience I can say that an assertiveness training course does not try to push people into something too deep for them. The task facing most teachers is to keep participants out of heavyweight situations and encourage them to practise first with the lightweight problems until they have developed enough confidence to tackle the more difficult ones. What the fearmongers ignore because they rarely comment from first-hand, personal experience, is the important parallel process which is occurring throughout the course. All the while you are looking at areas of your life which are sensitive, you are learning skills to handle these situations, so it is from a strengthened position that you can begin to look at these issues. And since any kind of change involves some kind of upheaval, even if only temporary, it is quite normal to need time to make readjustments.

Assertiveness training is neither better nor worse than therapy – it is different. For example, insight into why I behave as I do with male authority figures can be invaluable but insight falls short of helping me to learn the actual skills to behave differently in the real situation.

It's also important never to underestimate the effect that increased self-confidence can have in a person's life. If participants learn through personal role-play that they can change their behaviour, they learn to be more self-directed. Instead of being so dependent on outside advice, each person is working out for herself what she wants to do and say and this growth of self-esteem and self-reliance is a remarkable and powerful catalyst in many people's lives.

The final category of objections can be classified as ethical. Characteristic comments would be, 'You're teaching people to be selfish. What would the world come to if everyone thought only of themselves and never put themselves out for others?'; 'It's basically non-Christian to be self-centred because Christ taught that you should be passive.' This objection is rooted in a fundamental misunderstanding about assertiveness (i.e. that it means being selfish) and also in what appears to be an extraordinary blindness to the kind of world in which most of us live. I do not see a world where values such as care for the most vulnerable, consideration of others less fortunate than oneself, equality, honesty or truth are much in evidence. Assertiveness emphasizes the *quality* of human relationships. It is aggression which is blind to others in the quest for self-expansion and conquest. Assertive communication includes a consideration of how others are affected by your remark or gesture; it means considering what others want, and balancing that with being true to yourself. Certainly assertiveness offers a different set of values. But I am not convinced that more attention to these values would make the world a *worse* place.

In general, these objections are repeated most loudly by people who know of assertiveness training indirectly. Sometimes they have had an unfortunate encounter with a colleague or friend who 'turned' assertive on them and they didn't like the result. Unfortunately this can happen. It is easy for someone after a lifetime's experience of passivity to use assertive skills in an aggressive and often punishing way, in a spirit akin to revenge!

Striking the balance between ourselves and others is a continuing challenge. Many women are aware of going from one extreme to the other and slipping from passive to aggressive behaviour. We need to be watchful of this possibility, especially with people close to us as they frequently come in for heavy-handed treatment. The skills are powerful and need to be used with sensitivity. Self-disclosure, for example, is a very powerful technique in a culture used to the denial of emotions. Sometimes it can come as quite a shock to the other person and we need to remember this, not as a reason for not using it but certainly as a safeguard against using it as a weapon to settle old scores.

It is also important to consider what women have themselves reported, those who have attended a class, who have continued to practise the skills and who endeavour to put the principles into practice in their lives. First, we cannot avoid some losses. Learning to say no and set limits will mean that some relationships will founder if they cannot sustain change. Sometimes a woman will have the strength to terminate a relationship she has wanted to end for some time but could only talk about before. Assertiveness can be unfairly blamed for all sorts of relationship difficulties: 'It all started when you went on that bloody course!' is a characteristic comment in such a situation.

On the other hand, many women report that relationships have improved because they themselves are being clearer and more honest. There is often a period of uncertainty especially if, say, you have relied heavily on a little-girl image to get what you wanted in the past. As one woman said, she knew a lot of people were attracted to that little girl and was anxious about how they would respond but gradually got accustomed to being more adult and feeling better about herself. Other people may well delight in your changes and only be less accepting if their regard for you is dependent on your staying as you were. It is also true that some women find themselves getting very impatient with people who won't be specific and with relationships and attitudes which now seem restrictive.

Although the skills continue to be useful long after a class has ended, women often express ambivalence. There is certainly an ongoing sense of pride and achievement in handling situations more effectively but there are moments when every one of us wishes we had never heard of assertiveness! Life before assertiveness training assumes a rosier hue in those moments when we fondly remember how much easier things were before we learned to acknowledge responsibility for our own behaviour; how much easier it used to be when we could just blame everybody else! Asserting yourself is a *daily* choice and there are many occasions when you may think 'I really don't have the energy today to take it on,' and so let something pass. What matters is that you are making a choice: whether or not you use the skills at all or use them effectively, you always learn something, even from mistakes.

So what are the long-term advantages? My own experience, and I know this is echoed by thousands of other women, is a more rewarding and fulfilling life. You can begin to live more reflectively

165

than reactively, thinking and considering more than responding instantly on the defensive. Without becoming self-obsessed, you can learn a lot about yourself, and learn to be remarkably honest with yourself because your self-esteem is more strongly rooted. When you fall down, as one woman described it, there is a safety net so you don't fall right through and you can pick yourself up more easily. Many women report that assertiveness can be picked up by 'osmosis' – that partners and children acquire the skills by example, learning to be specific about what they want, to set limits, to express feelings much more clearly themselves.

This brings me to the wider implications of assertiveness training. After ten years of involvement with the subject I am as committed as ever because it has grown with me from a set of communication skills to certain beliefs which are very important to me personally. This does not mean I will always behave or even think assertively but it offers me, and others, a way of being in this world. For me assertiveness offers hope. Because it is based on self-esteem, it offers a new way of relating to other people. The power that is released when individuals stop hating themselves is a potentially remarkable force for change. We are less afraid to make contact with others whose lives and values are very different because we can move from a centred sense of self. As we free ourselves from the tyranny of self-hatred we can contribute to that process of liberation in others and acquire the necessary humility and wisdom to recognize both our individuality and interdependence as women in this world.

Index

Further Reading

(all in paperback)

Your Perfect Right, Robert Alberti and Michael Emmons, Impact, 1974

Self Assertion for Women, Pamela Butler, Harper and Row, 1976

The Assertive Woman, Stanlee Phelps and Nancy Austin, Impact, 1975

When I say No I feel Guilty, Manuel Smith, Dial, 1975

Women's Rights: A Practical Guide, Anna Coote and Tess Gill, Penguin, 1977

The Cinderella Complex, Colette Dowling, Fontana, 1982

How to Survive as a Working Mother, Lesley Garner, Penguin, 1982

Fat is a Feminist Issue, Susie Orbach, Hamlyn, 1978

Our Bodies, Ourselves, Angela Phillips and Jill Rakusen, Penguin, 1978

Treat Yourself to Sex, Paul Brown and Caroline Faulder, Penguin, 1979

My Secret Garden, Nancy Friday, Quartet, 1973

The Hite Report, Shere Hite, Dell, 1976

The Body Electric, Ann Hooper, Virago, 1980

Sex for Women, Carmen Kerr, Grove Press, 1977

For Ourselves, Anja Meulenbelt, Sheba, 1981